MW0129O387

Foreword

There is widespread opinion at the Pentagon that the United States of America rules supreme over land, sea and sky on this planet. Now all that remains is to gain the same military supremacy in outer space. In our modern times all warfare is dependent on satellites. Development of military capacity in outer space has top priority at the Pentagon, regardless of whether the President is called Bill Clinton, George W. Bush or Barack Obama. Other countries follow suit accordingly. In recent years Norway has established satellite ground stations on Svalbard and in the Antarctic that are employed in conflicts and wars across the entire planet. The Svalbard Treaty prohibits the use of the archipelago *"for war-like purposes"*. The Antarctic Treaty states that the continent shall be *"used for peaceful purposes only"*.

Norway is currently engaged in the war in Afghanistan, side by side with the USA and other allies, a war that is difficult particularly because the enemy hides in areas impenetrable to most forms of ground or air-based surveillance. Photographs taken by satellites of these areas are of such high quality that it is possible to chart which roads and airbases have been used by the Taliban. Data from the satellites is downloaded on Svalbard. Is it realistic to assume that these photos are not put to use in Norwegian and allied warfare?

This is a story I would have preferred if possible not to have written. I know this book will cause problems for many heads of industry, military leaders and politicians. They can also expect to have to field awkward questions. For my part, I must be held accountable for my claims. At the same time, I feel I have a duty to write this story. Many a winter's evening I have stood outside my home in Vadsø, gazing at the cobalt heavens above and thought: "Are we to destroy this as well?"

As happens so often in life, random events awaken one's interest, which is how I first became involved in all this. It started with a journalist colleague of mine, Inge Sellevåg, who works for the Norwegian daily broadsheet Bergens Tidende, reading a notice in 1998 in the newspaper Aftenposten that the Norwegian Armed Forces were to install high-technology radar in Vardø to map space debris.

Sellevåg doubted that the radar would only be utilized in connection with charting space debris, and contacted several internationally renowned experts who confirmed the Vardø radar is a component of the controversial U.S. missile defense system against nuclear missiles. I read the sensational articles in Bergens Tidende, interviewed several of the American experts by telephone and produced news stories for the regional news channel NRK Finnmark. My interest had been kindled.

In the seventies and eighties Norwegian journalists and authors delved into American archives. They had to resort to the phone book to find out facts about military activity in Norway. Nowadays it's much simpler. When I started using the Internet to investigate the exact purpose of the

Vardø radar, I discovered many who are/were connected in some way to the Vardø radar that for reasons of their own, post information on the net. These include all the American companies that supplied equipment for the radar system and that are keen to showcase technical capabilities as a way to drum up new business. Then there are the U.S. military units eager to draw attention to their military import as a way to obtain funding. Last but not least, there is a 'forest' of American researchers working on military issues, also eager for the spotlight.

Moreover, the attitude towards openness in U.S. administration is totally different from the Norwegian. This means for instance that I was much better able to track the development of the radar system in Vardø through American Congress budgets than via information from the Norwegian Ministry of Defense.

I am in mild shock when the reality dawned on me that the "facts" I was presented with by Norwegian defense ministers and parliamentary secretaries did not match up with comprehensive documentation on the net and statements made by recognized researchers.

In 2005, Pål Sommer-Erichson and I made an investigative documentary for the TV program "NRK Brennpunkt" on the Vardø radar with new documentation verifying that the radar is used by the U.S. Missile Defense Agency. While working on the documentary I realize I still haven't quite got to the bottom of why the world's most advanced radar of its kind has been moved from California to Vardø. The answer to the question of why the Pentagon was so engaged in using radar to monitor objects over the

Equator still eludes me. I find this exceptionally irritating.

I continue to burn the midnight oil searching the Internet. It doesn't take too long for the truth to dawn on me: The most important function of the Vardø radar is its place in the development of a totally new weapons system, namely the defense of American and its allies' satellites and attack systems against enemy satellites. This is happening at the same time as the Chinese shoot down one of their own satellites in 2007, proving for the first time that they are capable of participating in a war in space. Six months later the Americans follow up, repeating the exercise.

Ståle Hansen, one of Norway's most competent journalists where military issues are concerned, encouraged me to take a closer look at Svalbard, which I did. Paragraph 9 of the Svalbard Treaty, which regulates the international status of the archipelago, states: "Norway undertakes not to create nor to allow the establishment of any naval base in the territories specified in Article 1 and not to construct any fortification in the said territories, which may never be used for warlike purposes".

I employ some of the key words I had used in my research on the Vardø radar, and suddenly very many doors swing open. It is 13 years since the first data was downloaded from satellites that could be used for warlike purposes. Since then things have progressed at breakneck speed with regard to number of satellites in operation for military purposes that utilize Svalbard, the military function for these satellites and the number of countries that have benefited in a military sense from the downloading of data from and control of the satellites from Svalbard.

Scouring the Internet for information about Svalbard also led me to contact one of Norway's foremost experts on Norwegian Svalbard-Policy. Geir Ulfstein, Professor of Law at the University of Oslo, who drew my attention to that the Antarctic Treaty has even stricter regulation of military activity in Antarctica than the Svalbard Treaty has in the north. In the treaty Norway and a number of other countries – including the USA – committed to engaging solely in peaceful activities on the continent.

To my amazement I discover several clear breaches of the treaty. The new Norwegian satellite station downloads surveillance pictures from two satellites, both of which have the American National Geospatial Intelligence Agency – NGA – as their most significant customer. The Norwegian station will also control and download data from the new European Global Navigation Satellite Galileo, which has both a civil and a military function.

The research into the Antarctic and Galileo brings me back to Europe again. The EU has a very active space policy, both civil and military. Galileo, which is currently under development, is the largest infrastructure initiative undertaken so far in the EU. The Norwegian Parliament has unanimously given its approval to participate in all stages of Galileo's construction, including the military function. Another factor that gives room for thought is that Galileo is being developed at the same time as a completely new European surveillance system, where once again Svalbard and the Antarctic play key roles. Private European companies, such as the Kongsberg Group, are participants in planning the EU's military capacity in outer space. The EU is in the process of planning military systems to defend its own and to attack hostile satellites, parallel with the U.S. Defense systems, of which the Vardø radar forms part.

Satellite overview

Satellite	Svalsat	Trollsat	Owner	Task
		Permission Use		
Landsat 5	Yes		USA	Earth observation
Landsat 7	Yes		USA	Earth observation
Terra	Yes		USA	Earth observation
Radarsat-1	Yes	Yes	MDA, Canada	Earth observation
Radarsat-2	Yes	Yes	MDA, Canada	Earth observation
DMSP satellites	Yes		USA	Meteorological observation
NPP	Yes		USA	Meteorological observation
Formosat-2	Yes		Taiwan	Earth observation
Kompsat-2	Yes		South Korea	Earth observation
TES	Yes		India	Earth observation
Cartosat-1	Yes		India	Earth observation
Cartosat-2	Yes		India	Earth observation
Iridium	Yes		Iridium, USA	Communication
RapidEye	Yes		RapidEye AG, Germany	Earth observation
COSMO-SkyMed	Yes		Italy	Earth observation
TerraSAR-X	Yes		Germany	Earth observation
GeoEye-1		Yes	GeoEye, USA	Earth observation
WorldView-1		Yes	DigitalGlobe, USA	Earth observation

WorldView-1		Yes	DigitalGlobe, USA
	Earth observation		
Galileo	Yes	Yes	EU
	Earth observation		

Content

CHAPTER 1
MEETING WITH SVALBARD

The stark, white domes are visible before one sees the airstrip and buildings in Longyearbyen. From the air they look like snowballs. 10–20 of these are spread across a naked mountain plateau. In the vast Arctic landscape they appear quite small. Steep, bare, rock faced mountains and the open sea surround the plateau.

This is the closest I get to the satellite station Svalsat. After landing I take a taxi into Longyearbyen. I find that the road up to the plateau is closed off with a barrier.

I telephone Station Manager Sten-Christian Pedersen and ask if it is possible to have a guided tour. I explain I am writing a book about Norwegian space activities, and am flexible about possible times to meet up. I am turned down immediately with: "Impossible, we have other priorities."

"But isn't there supposed to be open policy about the plant? I was given to understand..." "No, it's not possible," Pedersen cuts in, giving me no chance to offer new arguments. "We have other priorities. We have a fault with the transmission equipment; that has priority." With that, the telephone conversation was over.

Anyone who works at the station must have Norwegian Armed Forces and NATO security clearance.[1] Secret security measures have been implemented.[2] A public report from 2006 asserts that consideration must be given to the implementation of new security measures if Svalsat is connected to the European navigation system Galileo, a move that has now been approved for the station. The national security authority has been allocated

---

[1] Positions vacant, Kongsberg Satellite Services
[2] The Governor of Svalbard

9

responsibility for this.[3] Galileo's planners want soldiers stationed at the plant. Considerable pressure has in fact been applied on Norway to make this happen – although at the time of writing Norway has not acceded.[4]

9am, 3rd November 2010, I have an appointment with the Deputy Governor of Svalbard, Lars Fause. Fause has a reputation in journalistic circles as being an open and well-informed chap. Somewhat expectant I step out from the hotel and walk the few hundred meters to the Governor's building. I look up at the dark blue Arctic sky, but try as I may I cannot see any of the numerous satellites speeding overhead. The extreme cold makes the ground crunch under my feet.

I spy a large, grey-white, shaggy animal standing motionless at the edge of the road; I jump involuntarily. Luckily not a polar bear, but a Svalbard reindeer – sometimes mistaken for a small musk ox. It has found some tufts of grass sticking up through the snow. This reminds me I'm a long way north in the world, and the reason why the satellite industry is so interested in Svalbard.

The meeting starts nine o'clock on the dot. Fause is smiling and friendly, and offers coffee in his office. He is dressed in a suit and tie, as befits an officer of the Crown in this furthest outpost of the Kingdom. An experienced lawyer; he has correct observance of the Svalbard Treaty as one of his areas of responsibility. The treaty states categorically that the archipelago *must never be used for war-like purposes*. Fause is taken up with that the Svalbard Treaty must be understood and interpreted in terms of the time and context in which it was created, namely as a result of negotiations between the victor nations after World War I in Versailles, France.

3

https://www.nsm.stat.no/upload/Publikasjoner/%C3%85rsmeldinger/NSM%20%C3%A5rsmelding%202009.pdf , page 31, 18.04.11
[4] Central sources in the Ministry of Foreign Affairs

"You have to view the treaty from an historic perspective. Millions had been killed. It was vital to stipulate in the treaty that war should be avoided in the world, and that Svalbard should not and must not be utilized in a military sense was a natural reaction to and consequence of this. I believe that this was firmly imprinted in the minds of the negotiators gathered round the table in 1920. So history is an extremely important factor here. That's why paragraph 9 is in the treaty," says Fause.

Historic lines with significance for understanding the tension surrounding the military use of Svalbard today stretch far into the future, as well as centuries back in time, first and foremost in relation to our mighty neighbor to the east, Russia.

Russian researchers claim it was the Russians that first made use of the archipelago, a viewpoint that has traditionally provided grounds for claiming rights. Russian researchers claim that their landsmen were hunting reindeer, whales and bears on the archipelago as early as the eleventh or twelfth century.[5]

What many consider to be the first international clarification on the rights to Svalbard, dates from 1871 – an exchange of notes that was the predecessor to today's Svalbard Treaty.[6] There were plans for Norwegian settlement for part of the year, Norway claimed Norwegian sovereignty, but Russia opposed this. In 1871 it is evident that Svalbard is an open international territory.

The Svalbard Treaty of 1920 established full Norwegian sovereignty over the archipelago, but the agreement also commits Norway to a number of distinct, international obligations. The preamble to the treaty stipulates that the Islands must only be used

---

[5] Legal Regime of Maritime Space Adjacent to Spitsbergen, Professor Alexander N. Vylegzhanin, Professor Vyacheslav K. Zylanov
[6] Trygve Mathisen, *Svalbard i internasjonal politikk 1871–1925 (Svalbard in International Politics)*

11

for peaceful purposes, and Article 9 states that Svalbard "may never be used for warlike purposes". The Soviet Union's - and now Russia's - view has always been, and still is, that this classifies Svalbard as a demilitarized area.[7]

The Soviet Union did not participate in the negotiations on Svalbard in Versailles, and did not sign the Svalbard Treaty in 1925. At that time the Soviet Union was still opposed to Norwegian sovereignty over Svalbard, but signed the agreement in return for Norway's recognition of the new regime in Moscow.[8] Many Russians still regard Svalbard as a part of Russia.

The two fiber cables from Svalsat to the mainland have almost unlimited capacity to carry data from satellites to customers across the entire globe. Fause confirms there is no control over content in the flow of data, but he wishes there was: "If the police aren't out patrolling on the roads, a lot goes on that begs attention. It's much of the same in this instance", says Fause with a grin.

"You don't check the fiber cable at all. Maybe you should take a look, at least now and again?" I ask.

"Yes, that's correct", replies Fause. He goes on to say that the Norwegian Post and Telecommunications Authority (NPT) had taken the initiative to discuss the possibility of checking the flow of data, but thus far no concrete measures have been taken.

The most important factor in Soviet and later Russian Svalbard policy has been that Svalbard must not be utilized by Norway and other Western countries in a military context. The Soviet Union maintained Norway's participation in NATO's joint command system "North Atlantic Command" – that included Svalbard – was a clear breach of the Svalbard Treaty. In 1951 the Soviet Union wrote several harsh notes to Norway, which among

---

[7] Ambassadør Sergey Vdimovich, The Russian Embassy in Oslo

[8] Willy Østreng, *Det politiske Svalbard*, page 33 *The political Svalbard*

12

other things alleged that Norway must take full responsibility for the outcome of such a policy.

In 1958 Soviet Union again reacted vehemently. At the time there were plans to build an airport at Ny-Ålesund that would be open all year round. The Soviet Union feared that an airport could be used in a military connection, and also got wind of that ground surveys were to be partially financed by U.S. military authorities. The then Norwegian Minister of Foreign Affairs Halvard Lange wrote in a reply that the Norwegian Government had taken the necessary steps to stop the foreign financing for the Norwegian plans.

Svalbard's military significance for Russia has historically been linked to two circumstances: Firstly that the sea route between Finnmark (County) and Svalbard is Russia's securest thoroughfare to the world's seas in the west. Secondly, the fear that the geographic proximity to Russia would be utilized in any attack against Russia.

It was the last circumstance that precipitated the first protest by the Soviet Union in 1965 against Norwegian satellite activity on Svalbard. The previous year the European Space Agency (ESA) had received approval from the Norwegian Government to establish a station to send and receive signals from satellites. Soviet Union Prime Minister Kosygin writes to Norwegian Prime Minister Gerhardsen that the Soviet Union believes the station has a military potential, while Gerhardsen replies that the station does not have a military mission. The Soviet Union does not accept this at face value, and on April 30th 1969 the Soviet Government sends a memorandum to the Norwegian Government:

> The Soviet Government still believes the telemetry station on Svalbard, besides the purely scientific purposes, can be used for military purposes, particularly for the execution of cosmic, radio-technical and other forms for intelligence objectives over the territories of the Soviet Union, and that

the true propensity can only be determined by constant supervision and control of its operation by Soviet experts.[9]

The station was shut down five years later.

When once again interest for steering and downloading data from satellites took off at the end of the eighties, a separate regulation was created, the purpose of which was to ensure that the satellite activity is not in conflict with the Svalbard Treaty. This states that satellite owners and operators must apply to the NPT before they can utilize Svalbard. The Governor of Svalbard is responsible for checking that the terms and conditions of the permits are complied with.

Svalbard remains a bone of contention between Norway and Russia. The best-known conflict amongst the general public is the fishing rights and control over fishing in the waters off the archipelago, but the issues concerning military installations also pop up at regular intervals. The United States, Norway's chief ally, has been critical of Norwegian Svalbard policy, and has sympathy for that Russia as a military super-power is eager to wield influence in the area.

The Governor only has one lawyer that can spend 50 percent of his/her time on checking satellite activity on Svalbard. The Governor does not have separate technical expertise to be able to check on downloading and the control of a hundred or so satellites. The Governor must rely on the Norwegian Defense Research Institute (FFI), to assess the military significance. It thus boils down to the question of whether the FFI has the necessary independence. The FFI and the Norwegian Armed Forces use military data from several satellites that are controlled from Svalbard. The satellites include the Canadian satellites Radarsat-1 and Radarsat-2. Radarsat-2 was employed to prepare a map during the NATO exercise "Cold Response" conducted in Troms during the winter of 2009. The exercise was used as the final preparation for Danish military forces before they were shipped out to

---

[9] Translation of a Soviet memorandum, 30th April 1969

14

Afghanistan. The Royal Norwegian Navy has used data from Radarsat-1 for many years.

Lars Fause says the Svalbard Treaty sets limits on the type of military activity permitted when using Svalsat: "What we are engaged in Afghanistan I would in a legal context – I emphasize: in a purely legal context – consider as war purposes".

Fause also says it is a problem in relation to the Svalbard Treaty to use satellite information to train Norwegian soldiers who are going to Afghanistan, or for NATO exercises in Northern Norway. Clearly, this qualified lawyer is uncomfortable with having to sit with responsibility for the inspectoral tasks. For close to a decade now the Ministry of Transport and Communications has had plans to renew the regulations, but to date no revision has been initiated.

The Governor still carries out two pre-advised visits to Svalsat annually to check which satellites the station communicates with, without any form of inspection to ascertain content of the flow of data. This is the current mode of inspection. Meanwhile the flow of traffic and the technology have progressed at an alarming rate.

During the first few years of satellite activity data was transmitted from satellites to ground stations, re-transmitted to sender satellites and then down-streamed to the final recipients. This method of data transfer was costly. The Pentagon funded the laying of two fiber cables from Svalbard to the mainland in 2003.[10] This connection is capable of dealing with all U.S. e-mail traffic for a year in the space of six minutes. It takes milliseconds to transfer data from Svalbard to customers all over the world. Fause says inspection of this is far from satisfactory:

---

[10] http://edocs.nps.edu/npspubs/scholarly/MBAPR/2006/Jun/06Jun_Buchanan_M BA.pdf

15

"A report from the NPT pointed to four alternatives that would provide a more stringent inspectorate than that currently in practice. There perhaps lies the answer in a political discussion of which kind of inspectorate is preferred. The answer must be determined by those who sit and decide this", says Fause.

The man who holds a key position for ensuring Norway's commitments in regard to the Svalbard Treaty are upheld says – albeit indirectly – that the extent to which satellite activities are checked is highly inadequate.

Once back at the hotel I had no problem in connecting to the Internet. No complaints either about connection speed, thanks to satellite activity! I lie on my bed and enter "Pathfinder" and "Svalbard" in Google's search field. Pathfinder is the name of a magazine published by the National Geospatial-Intelligence Agency (NGA), one of the six U.S. military intelligence organizations. I have read the article on NGA's visit to Norway before, but I feel the need to read it again:[11]

It's a chilly day in late August 2007 and a foreign delegation arrives on a day's visit to Svalbard. Many foreign groups visit Svalbard, but this one is special. These are the top bosses of U.S. military intelligence. They are on a three-day visit in Norway to further develop the cooperation between the United States and Norway.

Jack Hill leads the delegation. He is one of the directors in NGA. In Oslo they are informed on Norwegian military intelligence efforts from the Arctic region to Afghanistan. Two of the three days are spent in the north of Norway. The group visits Svalsat, are informed on all aspects of the activity, and are most impressed. Hill says Norway can point to world-class results.

I scroll up and down in the article. As with all articles intelligence services upload (for public viewing) about their

---

[11]

https://www1.nga.mil/Newsroom/Pathfinder/0602/Pages/NorwayDemonstrates GEOINT.aspx activities, there is little concrete information about military capacities and military tasks.

I ask myself: Is it possible to gain an overview of military activity on Svalbard? Is there irrefutable evidence that Norway is violating the Svalbard Treaty? What does Russia and other countries have to say? Is Norway involved in the militarization of outer space? Where do I begin?

Chapter 2

A matter for TV news and Parliament

Saturday 15 February and Sunday 16 February 2003 are red-letter days for peace activists in many countries. That's when a demonstration is held of a kind never before seen in the world, against the United States' imminent plan to invade Iraq. An estimated ten million people march in processions in 800 cities in more than 60 countries.

In Rome over a hundred buses and many trains are hired to transport people to the center of the city. The majority of those wanting to express their abhorrence are nonetheless unable to reach the main venue due to the massive hordes of people. It is estimated three million are out in the streets of Rome, and the Guinness Book of Records claims the demonstration is the biggest anti-war demonstration ever held.

The demonstrations in Norway also smash all previous records. 60 000 people stand packed together like sardines in a tin in Youngstorget in Oslo. Labour Party's Trond Giske, Liberal SV's Kristin Halvorsen and Bishop Gunnar Stålsett hold rousing speeches: "The world is standing on the brink of war. We are demonstrating our will for peace. Therefore we are mobilizing our greatest force: The strength of human fellowship, the spirit of peace and the power of our conviction", thunders Stålsett in his address to the sea of faces before him.[12]

National TV NRK's anchorman Petter Nome, who compares Bush to Hitler, is one of the front figures in the event.

A total of 130 000 people – young and old - take part nationwide. It's not every day that Norwegians march in such numbers in protest demonstrations: 1700 in Bodø, 20 000 in Trondheim and 700 in Elverum.

---

[12] http://www.aftenposten.no/nyheter/uriks/article491023.ece

Prime Minister Kjell Magne Bondevik turns the U.S. President down flat when he phones, calling for Norway's support. An opinion poll shows that nine of ten Norwegians are against the American invasion plans.

But then you have to wonder; did Norway keep as much out of the war as the country had officially committed to. The fact is that Svalbard Satellite station, Svalsat, had immense significance for the entire invasion.

A document I found on the net is particularly interesting because it recounts Svalbard's military significance when U.S. tanks rolled in towards Baghdad and U.S. bombers took off from their bases.

The document, which was authored by researchers at the U.S. Naval Research Laboratory is called, "The mission support role played by MODIS during Operation Iraqi Freedom".[13] MODIS stands for Moderate Resolution Imaging Spectroradiometer, and is an advanced instrument on the NASA satellites Terra and Aqua. In terms of military use the instrument can produce images capturing valuable information on height of the cloud base, description of fires and not least – the development of sandstorms.

In Afghanistan in 2001 U.S. pilots were taken unawares by desert dust and sandstorms. This led to inaccurate navigating, bombs didn't hit their targets and innocent people became the victims. The Pentagon determined to be better prepared for the next war, and commenced work on utilizing satellite pictures from civil satellites of sandstorms and high concentrations of desert dust.

In particular, the MODIS instrument on NASA satellites was regarded as a highly valuable asset in predicting sandstorms.

---
[13] http://www.informaworld.com/smpp/content~db=all~content=a747979843, 18.04.11

The problem however was that it took one to two weeks to get the data from satellites to the front, while the generals maintained the data had to reach there in the space of two or three hours if it was to have any significance for choice of attack target and weaponry. The U.S. Air Force, U.S. Navy and NASA collaborated on finding a solution. A crucial part of the solution was the downloading of data at Svalbard, where it was immediately sent via a communications satellite to the United States for processing and then sent on to Iraq.

It transpires that the new satellite pictures have decisive significance for the American invasion forces in Iraq. Three days after the onset of the invasion a sandstorm grounded all U.S. Air Force aircraft. The sandstorm is the most powerful for several years. All back up for the ground forces must now come from the Navy. The entire operation is in danger of stalling.

Specialists at the Naval Research Laboratory retain contact with leading officers on U.S. aircraft carriers out in the Gulf. MODIS takes on a major role. Commander Anthony Wade on the aircraft carrier "USS Abraham Lincoln" says: "The Navy is now taking over all support functions for the ground forces. The air force has halted its operations. All ships are now receiving aircraft, also from other aircraft carriers. We are now employing the (MODIS) products to determine how the aircraft carrier can provide secure support for the operation."

Commander Steven Cole on the aircraft carrier "USS Kitty Hawk" is equally satisfied: "We are checking the products twice a day … thank you for the support, it's crucial for us out here. We are employing the (MODIS) products to assess sandstorms over Iraq, and it's an impressive product".

I seek out the e-mail address to the researcher Steve D. Miller, who is the principal author of the report to the Naval Research Laboratory. December 21 2009 I ask him to confirm the contents of the report and ask if it is possible to do a TV interview with him. I receive a reply the same day, where among other things he writes:

"I understand you are interested in how Svalbard was utilized to receive MODIS in close to real time, the data from which was subsequently used to support operations in conflicts in the Middle East."

This is irrefutable confirmation of the report's contents. However I am not immediately successful in clinching an interview. He refers to others. However, just after the New Year I get a break. Researcher Jeff Hawkins writes to me and says he can front up. He writes about the significance of MODIS: "Due to high definition images and good weather reports, the forces managed to deal with the storm in relatively sheltered locations until the storm died down … our products are used in actual operations in Iraq and in Afghanistan."

I'm beginning to look forward to a trip away from the Polar darkness in Finnmark to sunny California. A few weeks later my plans are brought to an abrupt halt. Hawkins has got cold feet.

"Hi Bård, I have a written response working its way through the public release mill, but in the meantime I've decided a TV interview is not desired. You want someone to show how the Svalbard satellite reception capabilities directly assist "allied" operations in Iraq and Afghanistan from a military perspective. I don't want to be that spokesperson. There is no need to draw unwarranted attention to our efforts since there are more than a few unbalanced crazies on this planet."

He suggests that I instead interview him about Svalbard's significance for its ability to warn of tropical cyclones. I thank him but turn down his offer.

The parallel to the US Naval Research Laboratory in Norway is the Norwegian Defense Research Institute, FFI. After being shunted for long enough from pillar to post in the system to another, I give up. There are no independent civilian research milieus in this area in Norway. I have to travel abroad to find interviewees.

Shortly after I board a Widerøe aircraft in Vadsø and commence the journey to Groningen in Holland. I am due to meet with the Dutch researcher Frank Slijper who is attached to the Transnational Institute. This is a global civilian network of researchers who receive funding from both the European Commission (EC) and the Dutch Foreign Affairs Ministry.

I'm aware that I'm on edge as I travel this February day on the last stretch of the railway between Amsterdam and Groningen. Before me I see an endless panorama of dead-flat, but surprisingly snow-bedecked fields. I wonder if he will say the same as he said to me on the telephone. Will he confirm that Svalbard was important for American warfare in Iraq? Will he confirm a breach of the Svalbard Treaty? I'm almost at my destination.

First eye contact is friendly, the handshake firm. Slijper is a man in his early forties, and he invites me first to lunch at a tiny, packed lunch restaurant next door to his office in the center of Groningen. Slijper has recently published a book on Europe's military space policy, and is one of the most renowned researchers in this area in Europe.

"I am certain that Svalbard's significance for the U.S. invasion in Iraq is a clear breach of the Svalbard Treaty", says Slijper as we eat.

I start to relax a little, but not totally, at least not until he repeats the same words while the camera is rolling. On the train back to Amsterdam I can finally lean back and relax. Confirmation at last. What will the Russians say? It runs through my mind how the Norwegian authorities in Oslo and the long-serving ambassador in Moscow, Øyvind Nordsletten, have repeatedly assured the Russians that Svalsat is solely engaged in civilian and scientific activities.[14]

---

[14] http://www.ffi.no/no/Publikasjoner/Documents/FFI-Fokus-2004-1.pdf, page 7

"Come in. Come in", I hear a voice say in Norwegian – with just a hint of an accent - from a loudspeaker on the wall.

I have rung the doorbell to the Russian Embassy in Skillebekk, Oslo's most exclusive neighborhood. The neighborhood is typified by wide streets and imposing white villas framed by well-tended gardens. The door opens automatically.

To many of my colleagues' amazement I have been granted an interview appointment with the Russian ambassador to Norway. He has a reputation for very rarely giving interviews.

The cameraman and I enter. Suddenly it's like being in a government office building in Murmansk or Moscow. A spacious, bare reception room in subdued colors with an oblong window near a side room providing full view over everyone who enters and leaves the building. Stuffy air – just like I am used to from offices in Russia.

We are received by the voice from the loudspeaker, the man behind the voice proves to be the Russian ambassador's press liaison. We are expected, and are led to an adjoining room with lounge suites where we are invited to sit down and wait there for Ambassador Sergey Vadimovich Andreev.

The meeting with the Ambassador is far less formal than I had expected. I had sent questions in advance I meant were most significant to the interview, but after a short introductory conversation where I explain about my work so far, he makes it clear that I can interview him on all aspects of Norwegian satellite activity on Svalbard. He is worried about the Norwegian satellite activity, and stresses that Russia maintains that any military activity whatsoever on the archipelago is a breach of the Svalbard Treaty.

"If this information is correct, we must raise this with the signature countries. Our aim is to ensure that there is correct observance of the Svalbard Treaty", says Andreev. He asks to take

23

a closer look at my documentation that Svalbard is being utilized for war-like purposes.

My reportage is one of the main items in the news program Dagsrevyen on March 10, 2010. Three persons from the Norwegian Ministry of Foreign Affairs have viewed the item earlier that day, which was a somewhat unusual pre-condition Ministry officials insisted on if they were to comment. Arctic consultant Karstein Klepsvik is interviewed, and says it is data for weather forecasts that is downloaded on Svalbard, a practice that can in no way be a breach of the Svalbard Treaty. "Norway has always conscientiously complied with the Svalbard Treaty to the letter. We are clearly within the framework of the Treaty in downloading of data for weather reports", says Klepsvik.

I'm not expecting any major political epilogue. I have covered political security topics before without these having resulted in debate. This report however, is an awkward matter for the Norwegian government.

The next day the deputy leader for the Socialist Left Party (SV), Audun Lysbakken, is on the phone to me. He wants more information on the matter. It emerges that SV is not satisfied with the reply from the Ministry of Foreign Affairs.

SV takes the unusual step of requesting a written account to be presented in Parliament on the matter by the Minister of Foreign Affairs in the (coalition) government they themselves are a part of.

The reply from Jonas Gahr Støre contains little if anything new. It repeats that the satellite data from Svalbard has been utilized to prepare weather forecasts and that this is not a breach of the Svalbard Treaty. Støre writes he is of the opinion they are on safe legal ground.

SV accepts this explanation, and the matter once more quietens down.

Just a few searches in Google can result in a wealth of information. It emerges that the information that came from NASA satellites often decided whether the fighter aircraft should use laser or GPS-steered weapons.[15] If there was smoke or clouds over the target, a GPS bomber was selected instead of laser-steered weaponry that requires direct visibility.

The U.S. Naval Research Laboratory (NRL) websites relates that one year after the invasion of Iraq, researchers in the U.S. Navy who were responsible for the new flow of data to Iraq received an award for their efforts in connection with the "war on terror". The researchers received the award for having utilized satellite data that was essentially intended for research objectives for war efforts in Iraq. The grounds for the award were stated to be: "Operational personnel in the Navy and Air Force provided key information on the value of products that affected air operations positively, including targeting and choice of routes, choice of weapons/sensors and launches/landings from/on aircraft carriers".[16]

In his reply to Parliament to SV's inquiry, Minister of Foreign Affairs Jonas Gahr Støre nonetheless says quote: "the connection between the downloading of the actual data and military use of this is undoubtedly too remote and derivative".

I look at a photo of the U.S. Navy researchers who received an award for having used Svalbard (as an instrument) in the invasion of Iraq that a whole world opposed. They are smiling.

I find myself wondering if it's always like this, that whatever the Minister of Foreign Affairs tells Parliament is accepted without question as the truth, especially when the Minister of Foreign Affairs also happens to be Norway's most popular politician: Jonas Gahr Støre?

15
http://www.nrlmry.navy.mil/sat_training/nexsat/aux_files/SPIE_2004_Denver55 48-35_SATFOCUS_MillerEtAl.pdf, 14.04.11
16
http://www.nrlmry.navy.mil/headlines/headlines/news_archives/head_nasa.htm

Chapter 3
The new war

It all seems so peaceful. Two men sitting in front of computer screens inside a trailer at a military base a short drive from the casinos in Las Vegas. Both are clad in military uniforms. With the aid of satellites they have just taken over control of an unmanned aircraft in flight over Afghanistan.

On the other side of the globe, in the tiny village of Ali Khel in a Pakistani mountain region on the border of Afghanistan, it is a chilly, quiet November night in 2008, and all are asleep. An unmanned aircraft glides slowly, silently through the sky toward the rural town. The two men in the trailer in Nevada can see the dawn breaking over the village, thanks to a small video camera attached to the underside of the aircraft.

Inside the trailer they make final adjustments, bringing the aircraft on to the correct course for the target. One of them readies a laser-controlled partially Norwegian-manufactured Hellfire missile in the unmanned aircraft on the other side of the Atlantic. Seconds later two missiles are fired at a specific house in the village.

Western intelligence claims that Al-Qaida member Rashid Rauf, suspected of planning an attempted terrorist attack against Heathrow Airport in London in August 2006, was killed. Al-Qaida claim Rashid Rauf was not in the village, and that five innocent people were killed and several children injured.

Regardless it does not negate the fact that several people died, and several sustained injures in the village. Some of these were innocent victims. The two men in the trailer at the military base were able to go home to their families and carry on their lives as normal.[17]

---

[17] Based on various sources: "Hunting the Taliban in Las Vegas", *The Atlantic*, September 2006; "Droner. Fører krig fra en stol i Nevada" (Drones. Making war

The fact that one avoids own losses is one of the advantages with the new aircraft. They are also relatively economical and highly efficient. Afghanistan has proved to be the breakthrough point for Unmanned Aerial Vehicles, UAV.

The Pentagon now trains more pilots to sit in front of computer screens - far from the arenas of war – than sit in actual aircraft. It is estimated that the U.S. Air Force has the capacity to fly 50 unmanned aircraft simultaneously, four times the number possible three years ago. The unmanned aircraft are now a natural element of all major military operations in Afghanistan – for both armed attacks and surveillance. And it doesn't stop there: The Americans have plans to develop whole swarms of mini-aircraft that attack in unison, including unmanned bomber and fighter aircraft.

The Joint Strike Fighter, which Norway has decided to acquire, may end up being the last manned fighter aircraft. Development of unmanned aircraft has progressed at breakneck speed. The first time these aircraft were used in a specific role was during the fighting in the Balkans in the nineties, but then only as intelligence aircraft.[18]

This would not have been possible without the advances made in new satellite technology. The aircraft utilize communication satellites to transfer live images, control aircraft and fire missiles. The aircraft employ military GPS data, for among other things navigation and missile control and target location and identification. Observation and intelligence satellites are employed when planning sorties for selecting flight paths to glean information on hostile targets. "You can't go to war and win

---

from a chair in Nevada), *Aftenposten*, 22nd February 2010; "US missile kills UK militant in Waziristan", *The Nation*, 23rd November 2008 and "Top al-Qaeda terrorist Abu Zubair al-Masri 'was missile target in Bush campaign for favourable legacy'", *The Times*, 25th November 2008.

[18] Snooping on the Serbs, ABCNews.com

without space", is a well-known quote from a top-ranking officer in the U.S. Air Force, General Lance W. Lord.[19]

Satellites are now employed in absolutely all types of military operations. They have become a natural and necessary element in all military activity.[20]

It is now official that the Norwegian satellite station Svalsat, located on Svalbard, serves satellites employed for both military and civil purposes. Svalsat started with a few stumbling steps in 1997 together with one of the 'heavyweights' of the U.S. arms industry, Lockheed Martin. Svalsat now has agreements with around 100 satellites, and according to the company is the world's most active receiver station for earth observation, with customers across the globe. The Norwegian Armed Forces now utilize satellite data from Svalsat on a routine basis to monitor the Barents Sea and the Norwegian Sea. This is despite the fact only roughly 20 years have passed since the global defense industry woke up to the potential of the technology.

Satellites emerged as a vital component of modern warfare during the Kuwait War in 1991. Two official American evaluations of the war provide a rather exceptional insight into how technical innovations thousands of miles above the arena of war on the desert sands below were of fundamental significance for the Allied Forces success - after the invasion of Iraq – in hunting out Saddam Hussein's forces.[21] One document is 100 pages long, the other is ten pages, and both are authored by U.S. Space Command. Both documents are now declassified and accessible for public viewing in the U.S. National Archives.

At the outbreak of the war three U.S. satellites hang strategically placed over the Middle East. One of the three is moved to its position, 40 000 kilometers above the ground, just

---

[19] http://www.au.af.mil/au/awc/awcgate/space/afspc_almanac.pdf
[20] "Military uses of space", Parliamentary Office of Science and Technology, London, December 2006
[21] http://www.gwu.edu/~nsarchiv/NSAEBB/NSAEBB39/, document 7 and 10

before war erupts. They belong to the Defense Support Program-satellites, DSP, which in their time were built to warn of Russian nuclear attacks. The United States enters into cooperation with a ground station in Australia to transfer data quickly to the battlefield. The Americans fear Iraq's missiles, and are determined to be fully prepared.

Before the war Saddam Hussein's regime had acquired Scud missiles from the Soviet Union. Iraq fired these missiles at Israel and against U.S., British and other allied forces. It was essential to discover the launch sites of the Scud missiles. The three U.S. DSP satellites then utilize their light and heat sensors, enabling them to detect the launches, and send this information so that radar in Turkey can track the missiles' flight paths and provide positions to the American Patriot antiballistic missiles, which are immediately fired towards the incoming missiles. In the space of a few minutes the civilian population is also warned and they evacuate to the safety of air raid shelters.

An assessment from United Space Command says: "The cooperation between our space-based warning system and our antiballistic Patriot missiles was one of the great successes of the war."

But it isn't just early warning satellites that have surprisingly major significance for the war. A major breakthrough occurs for the military GPS system. The reason being that for large forces in desert areas it proves impossible to use regular maps, due to that there are no roads, rivers or mountaintops to use as landmarks. The soldiers discover the few GPS receivers that are available, are of immeasurable help. At the start of the war the U.S. forces have 500 GPS units; by the end there are 4500 receivers in tanks, vessels, aircraft and camps.

For the first time, satellite-based navigational, positioning and time management systems play a major and highly significant role in modern warfare. The following is an excerpt from the two declassified reports from the United States Space Command:

Fighter aircraft equipped with GPS could fly in under the protection of cloud cover and emerge again when they reached their targets. The navy used GPS to locate and remove mines and to provide co-ordinates for Tomahawk cruise missiles. [...] special operation units used GPS in much of their equipment.

Communication satellites also achieve a major breakthrough with the military operations. The Americans discover the telecommunications network is well developed in Saudi-Arabia, but not in Kuwait. Thus 90 percent of all communication goes to and from the battlefield with half a million soldiers engaged via satellite. The military communication satellites did not have sufficient capacity to deal with this volume of traffic. The Pentagon was totally dependent on civilian satellites.

The fourth class of satellite in the U.S. Space Command's review is the commercial earth observation satellites that orbit around the North and South Poles. In 1991 only the French Spot satellites and the U.S. Landsat satellites are on the market. During the war the Pentagon purchased data from Landsat and Spot for millions of dollars. Money spent so that the Pentagon could study the effects of bomb attacks, gain information on Iraqi troop movements and prepare better maps. Both Landsat and Spot have used Svalbard.[22] We will see that there are also a number of other satellite owners that have chosen Norway for the management and downloading of data.

The fifth type of satellites dealt with in the U.S. Space Command's review of the Gulf War are the meteorological satellites. The Americans have three separate military weather satellites that they call the Defense Meteorological Satellite Program, DMSP. The military also utilizes civilian satellites. The

---

[22] see Bo Andersen: "Med rommet som plattform – med øye for Jorda og den tredje dimensjon", (With space as the platform – and an eye on Earth and the Third Dimension) Norsk Romsenter (The Norwegian Space Centre) and http://www.ipgp.fr/pages/02050402.php?version=print&langue=1

U.S. Space Command maintain that data from the weather satellites played a key role in the warfare:

> The information was used extensively in planning and executing attack missions, determining wind direction and possible spread of chemical substances, and to warn U.S. forces of sandstorms and other weather conditions. Access to fresh data provides U.S. forces with the opportunity to use equipment to see in the dark and find targets with infrared instruments.

DMSP is still the only U.S. military satellite system for weather and environment data, and has now been extended by a number of new satellites.[23] The scope of use ranges from traditional weather forecasts to providing all types of environmental data. This for instance can concern data on visual conditions at sea, which could have significance for specialist forces, or the scope of smoke development that can be important when fuel storage plants etc. are set on fire. DMSP uses Svalsat, and there have been plans to make Svalsat one of the key ground stations for the next generation of U.S. weather satellites.[24] As we will see later, these plans were a crucial reason why a fiber cable was laid in to Svalbard.

The last category of satellites referred to by the U.S. Space Command is the intelligence satellites. Much of the report is devoted to these. However most of the pages are censored using a felt tip pen as the content is still considered classified.

It does however emerge that intelligence satellites have two main tasks in the war. One is to attempt to identify and locate the mobile launch ramps for the Scud missiles that can wreak such devastation. The other is to provide early warning of missile launches. Intelligence satellites can listen in on enemy communications, and also intercept civilian communications, as for example by wiretaps on telephones.

---

[23] http://www.af.mil/news/story.asp?id=123023558
[24] http://www.ipo.noaa.gov/IPOarchive/ED/Articles/EOM_Apr_May04.pdf

32

Immediately after the last dust clouds have settled in Kuwait, the Commander-in-Chief of the U.S. Air Force, General Merrill McPeak, holds a speech at the National War College where he examines the significance of satellites in warfare. He is crystal-clear about the significance of the war effort in space. He also calls the Gulf War "the world's first space war".[25]

Twelve years pass before the United States is once again at war in the Middle East. In the years between the Gulf War until the invasion of Iraq to overthrow Saddam Hussein the time is utilized by the U.S. Armed Forces to integrate satellites into the overall machinery of war. Researchers at Boeing also come up with something totally new: GPS-steered ammunition and GPS-steered bombs. In contrast to 1991 the United States is in 2003 well equipped to reap military benefits from its position as the undisputed leading space nation.

When the aging B-52 bomber aircraft take off for sorties during the invasion in 2003, the crew have intelligence data with images, threat assessments and target analyses that may have already undergone analysis at several locations elsewhere in the world. Nonetheless, the data is only a few seconds old.[26] The aircraft have exact coordinates to dangerous areas, making it a much easier task to plot safe routes to and from the combat area. They have exact position of targets, enabling the crew to release a GPS-steered missile. If threats arise or changes occur with the target while the aircraft is airborne, the control room can contact the aircraft at any given time and provide updated information. The crew also have an updated, precise weather forecast for the entire mission, and can likewise be contacted during the mission if the weather should change.

After the missiles are released, those on board can then provide information on bomb damage to all other units involved in

---

[25] http://www.au.af.mil/au/awc/awcgate/acsc/00-144.pdf , side 10
[26] http://www.csbaonline.org/wp-content/uploads/2011/03/2004.12.01-Revolution-in-War.pdf

33

the operation, for among other reasons to enable orders for repeat bombings of targets to be given if this is deemed necessary.

One concrete situation that illustrates how an extensive satellite network and new data flow are changing warfare is the bomb attack against Saddam Hussein 7th April 2003. This was an operation that according to the U.S. Air Force would have previously taken several days to execute from the start of planning to the actual bombing. Now it all happens within a half hour.

The headquarters of the U.S. forces receives a report from the CIA that Saddam Hussein, his two sons and other top party officials are gathered in a building at a popular restaurant in the exclusive neighborhood of Mansour in Baghdad. In the space of 30 minutes the precise geographic position for the building has been confirmed, the attack approved, the GPS data transferred to an AWACS surveillance aircraft that in turn transfers the information to a bomber aircraft circling over Iraq. Just twelve minutes later the building and bunker below are totally destroyed by four GPS-steered bombs. It transpired however that the Americans were too late, or that the information they had was incorrect. Only innocent civilians – including several children – were killed in the attack.

After the invasion it is clear that use of data via communication satellites has been quadrupled compared with the Gulf War. This is despite the fact that the U.S. force only numbered 350 000, while more than half a million American soldiers participated in the Gulf War. In addition to direct transfer of speech, text and other data via normal channels, satellites were also employed by command centers far away from the battlefield. They controlled combat situations directly and provided support to the Special Forces while they were in areas under the control of Saddam Hussein.

It also emerged that satellites had become highly crucial for enabling bombs and other missiles to hit their targets. In 1991 the laser was the only method employed to guide missiles and bombs, a method known as surgical warfare with precision weaponry. Twelve years later GPS-guided weapons had their breakthrough.

34

Precision, or guided, weapons accounted for ten percent of all weapons used by the United States in the Gulf War. During the invasion of Iraq 70 percent of the 15 000 discharged missiles, bombs, or other types of weapons were guided weaponry.

Saddam Hussein and his generals also understood the immense significance satellites had after Iraqi forces were hounded out of Kuwait in 1991. Iraq had learnt its lesson. Before the invasion in 2003 the country had purchased equipment from Russia that was designed to block GPS satellite signals. During the American invasion Iraq attempted to block GPS signals with six electronic jammers, but the equipment was rendered harmless by the U.S. Air Force in two night sorties before it could do any significant damage.[27] This is the first time in history that active counter measures were initiated against space war installations during a war.

The war also revealed that U.S. satellites were, to a totally different extent than during the previous encounter, capable of warning of hostile missile attacks. The defense system had been thoroughly and successfully tested in advance in order to detect and provide information on different types of missiles.

The Americans are aware there are many countries keen to catch up on their technological lead. Russia, China and India in particular have ambitious space programs.[28] The United States is well aware that other countries will undoubtedly make advances and shorten the technology gap.

Vice Admiral Lowell E. Jacoby, Director of the U.S. Defense Intelligence Agency, said at a Senate hearing in February 2003 that "… a number of states will develop precision attack capabilities roughly equivalent to what the U.S. fielded in the mid-1990s.", and that the spread of these weapons "…will increasingly

---

[27]

http://www.computerworld.com/s/article/79783/U.S._Army_awarded_contracts_to_Russian_GPS_jammer_vendor

[28] Space Security 2007

put our regional bases and facilities at risk."[29] Without a doubt this means new armament and a greater hazard that war will break out.

According to the highly respected database of the international Union of Concerned Scientists, there are now a total of 994 active satellites owned by authorities and companies in more than 100 countries.[30] More than 600 satellites are civilian, but increasing numbers of the civilian satellites are utilized for both civil and military purposes. More than 270 satellites are purely military satellites, and of these 104 are American.

According to a new report from the French analysis firm Euroconsult – which is used by the Norwegian Space Centre and many other countries' space travel authorities – the number of satellites will have more than doubled in the next ten years.[31] The military will be the most active.

Euroconsult says 50 countries will launch 808 satellites between now and the year 2020. The most active countries will be the United States, China, India, Japan, Russia and Israel. There is no reason to believe that the significance and role satellites have in warfare around the globe will taper off in the near future.

---

[29] http://intelligence.senate.gov/108161.pdf

[30] http://www.ucsusa.org/nuclear_weapons_and_global_security/space_weapons/technical_issues/ucs-satellite-database.html

[31] http://www.euroconsult-ec.com/news/press-release-33-2/37.html

Chapter 4
A Computer Entrepreneur looks to the North

A short, stocky, elderly figure in a grey suit is waving his left arm so energetically at me that his jacket appears to be taking flight, exposing his white shirt to full view. His other hand is holding a mobile phone to his ear. The aforementioned gentleman and I had previously arranged to meet in the center of Lillestrøm town at one o'clock and are now talking on the phone to agree on an exact venue.

There in the middle of Lillestrøm's main street, Storgata, on a quiet Friday morning in August stands the next to legendary research scientist and businessman Rolf Skår. An arresting sight – a few strands of white hair sticking straight up from an otherwise shiny, bald head, in contrast to a lush, grey moustache, the round head and the direct gaze that meets me – I immediately think Gyro Gearloose, and quiver in anticipation; what can I glean from this meeting? Will he be the one who reveals what's behind the veil surrounding Svalsat's brief history?

Skår is best known for being one of the three founders of Norsk Data – one of the truly gigantic Norwegian industry success stories. Founded in 1967, and the first Norwegian company to be listed on the stock exchange in both London and New York. Many maintain Norsk Data's computers were at that time the most advanced in the world for a large number of applications.

Less well known is that for most of the past 20 years he has played a key role in the development of the Norwegian space industry. This is an industry that has grown rapidly and that in 2009 achieved a turnover of NOK 5–6 billion, a very healthy increase of 14 percent on the previous year.[32]

Skår grew up on Karmøy, a small western Norwegian island where his parents made their living from a smallholding and fishing. His interest for things technical was wakened when the first tractor arrived on the island. He had already made up his mind by the time he was 13 that he would become a chartered engineer. He is now 71 years old, but still works full-time for the European Space Agency (ESA) in Paris.

We sit down at a table at Kokos café in Storgata. It's a place where locals meet over a cup of coffee, with white walls, large windows looking out on the pedestrian street, low, white sofa groups with large, violet cushions, a counter displaying cakes and a freezer full of Diplom ice cream.

He sits himself down with coffee, apple cake, and ice cream that melts while he talks. He starts at the very beginning:

"It's rather amusing that my first encounter with space travel occurred before the time with Norsk Data, and in fact was the prelude to the establishment of Norsk Data. The background for this was that while I was a student at the Norwegian Institute of Technology (NTH), I had participated in developing a new computer that was called SAM 1. In my first job at the Norwegian Defense Research Establishment (FFI) we were given the task of further developing this machine for Tromsø satellite station. This new machine, SAM 2, was so good that I took the new technology with me, left the Norwegian Defense Research Establishment (FFI) and established Norsk Data with two colleagues", says Skår

More than 20 years later – in the early nineties – Skår has long since departed from Norsk Data and the Norsk Data success story is history. Neither is the situation ideal at the Norwegian Space Centre, which is suffering from insufficient activity. There had been expectations that the section in the north, Tromsø satellite station, would be a leading download station for the increasing number of satellites passing over the North Pole. But the

---

[32] http://www.romsenter.no/Norsk/Industrihjelp/

anticipated flood of customers didn't eventuate. Tromsø is nonetheless the ground station for among others Europe's first radar satellite, ERS-1, a satellite that can see through cloud bases and in darkness, and which enables the Armed Forces to carry out surveillance of our large areas of ocean. Norwegian researchers, as the first in the world, use the data to detect oil spills at sea.[33] But the total activity is not enough to justify the cost. The Norwegian Space Centre is in need of a turnaround operation.

It's in this situation that Skår is elected as Chairman for the Norwegian Space Centre. But he is looking even further north:

"Ever since the sixties we have known that Svalbard is the best location for a ground station serving Polar-orbiting satellites. Satellites take about ninety minutes to circumnavigate the Earth, and with each orbit they move slightly east or westwards to capture images or collect data from the entire planet. But the path of the satellites is always over the North Pole and the South Pole. Only Svalbard is situated close enough to the North Pole to enable a ground station to download data from all flights overhead. Svalbard is a developed area with a stable population and an airport. It was an opportunity we just had to take advantage of," Skår says enthusiastically as he finishes off the little there is of his ice cream that hasn't yet melted in the sun.

Inadvertently, Skår receives a 'helping hand' from the other side of the Atlantic. July 1989, President George Bush launches his plans for U.S. space activities in a 25-year perspective.[34] Surprisingly, at that time he prioritized gaining more knowledge about the Earth rather than about the moon or other planets. His plan was to construct a unique satellite network costing between 15 and 30 billion dollars. The satellites would function together and provide better knowledge on climate changes, weather, forest and

---

[33] Birgit Strømsholm, "Radarsatellitter – kort historikk" (Radar Satellites - a brief history), http://ndla.no/nb/node/53305

[34] "NASA Plans a 'Mission to Planet Earth'", *The New York Times*, 25th July 1989.

farming growth, sea temperatures and sea currents. But not a word was uttered about military use.

NASA commences planning the launch of a number of new satellites designated for polar orbits, the Earth Observing System (EOS). At that time the Americans are on the lookout for the best sites from which to control the satellites and to download data. They consider an American research station in Antarctica and a site on Greenland.[35] A delegation from NASA is also on its way to Kiruna to look at Esrange Space Center, run by Norwegian Space Centre's counterpart in Sweden, Rymdaktiebolaget. News of this reaches the Norwegian Space Centre, and they decide to make the most of a possible opportunity to have Svalbard included in the contest:

"We ask the Americans straight out if they would also consider making a side trip to Svalbard, and it turns out they're a travel-happy bunch. The delegation travels to Longyearbyen together with some of our people. They are quickly convinced of the site's excellence. First and foremost because Svalbard, in contrast to all ground stations situated otherwise close to the North Pole, can communicate with satellites in all the 14 orbits a satellite completes around the Earth in the space of 24 hours. An easy decision that disappoints the Swedes", says Skår with a grin.

Skår takes a break to eat the slice of apple cake. I slurp cold coffee. I glance down at the page where I have written down questions I prepared the previous evening. I know I have to broach the difficult part now. I've already read in the annual reports for the Norwegian Space Centre that a new satellite station's relation to the Svalbard Treaty had been up for discussion. The Ministry of Foreign Affairs and the Ministry of Justice and Public Security had given its support to establish a satellite station on Svalbard. How could Skår be certain that operation of a satellite station wouldn't conflict with the terms of the Svalbard Treaty?

---

[35] http://en.scientificcommons.org/42760725

Rolf Skår immediately bridles, he squirms a little, and in contrast to his tone earlier, he replies brusquely: "This was the authorities' responsibility. We applied for permits, received permits and conducted ourselves accordingly. This was the authorities' responsibility. There's nothing more to say on the subject."

At this point in time the Norwegian Space Centre was a foundation and not a State organ as is the case today, and enforcement of the Svalbard Treaty was first and foremost the Ministry of Foreign Affairs' responsibility. I think to myself this is typically human to follow the formalities – shove the problems over on to others. The Norwegian Space Centre sat on technical expertise – not so with the Ministry of Foreign Affairs. Nonetheless I refrain from pursuing the question. I'm afraid it will lead to Skår becoming even more reticent with other information I am eager to obtain. There is no way he could have been ignorant of the gradual increasing significance Svalsat had for the military.

It emerges that no Norwegian voices were raised in criticism against the establishment on Svalbard.

Spring 1996, and the Norwegian Space Centre and NASA commence contract negotiations. The State Budget the same year allocates the first funding. In August NASA decides officially that the new ground stations for the planned satellites Aqua, Terra and the other satellites in the EOS programme will be sited at Longyearbyen on Svalbard and Poker Flat Research Range in Alaska. The satellites can be controlled and data downloaded during the 15 minutes they are visible from Svalbard before they pass the North Pole and are visible to a station in Alaska for another 15 minutes. The scene is now set for developments that will transform the Svalbard ground station into one of the world's most important communications centers.

The Tromsø firm *Barlindhaug Utbygging* immediately starts constructing a road up to the mountain plateau Platåberget, 450 meters above sea level, where the ground station is to be sited. In record time foundations for antennas and a plastic building

41

appear on the windswept plain. The Norwegian Space Centre and Ministry of Trade and Commerce pay the bill.

Soon after, a huge trailer from the United States turns up with technical equipment. The last stretch from Longyearbyen proves a nightmare for the fully loaded NASA truck. The new road isn't designed for such a large vehicle, and it only just manages to negotiate the tight bends up to Platåberget. From there the trailer drives into the plastic building built specially to provide protection against bad weather. The specialist vehicle serves as the operation center and as accommodation for the staff:

"This was a pioneering era. Our task was to man the station, and those who worked there had to live up there on the plateau for long periods of time, despite the weather not always being the best. Scrambling over high snowdrifts was part of everyday living. We were lucky enough to employ a Norwegian chartered engineer who had several winters behind him as a hunter on Svalbard. With his experience he had no trouble working and living isolated for long periods up on the plateau", said Skår.

The station is to be manned around the clock, and the Americans provide the training. The first antenna is erected. A connection is established with Isfjord Radio, which will send data to the communication satellites hovering at a fixed point 40 000 kilometers above the Equator. Due to the curvature of the Earth the signals must be directed southwards immediately above the ocean surface in order to communicate with receiver satellites. The communication satellites above the Equator send the data on to the United States. At Telenor there is widespread skepticism of the technical feasibility of this operation, but it does actually work. Thus the NASA *Isbjørn* - Polar Bear - Facility – as the Americans call the station on Svalbard – is a reality.[36]

Rolf Skår says the ground station was built to control and download data for the Terra, Aqua and Quickscan satellites, which are connected to NASA's new ambitious scientific EOS (Earth

---

[36] http://oiir.hq.nasa.gov/globablreach2008.pdf, page 81

42

Observing System) programme. But it is a Landsat satellite that becomes the first satellite that commences regular data downloads at Svalsat, with the launch of Landsat 7 from Vandenberg Air Force Base on 15th April 1999. This is stated in the parliamentary report on Svalbard from 1999. The Landsat programme has long been linked to the Pentagon, including as mentioned earlier during the Gulf War in 1991. I let Skår know I am aware which satellite was first to start using Svalsat. "Ah yes, the old 'workhorses'. But the decision to build Svalsat was linked to the EOS programme, all of which had scientific purposes", he says, and starts to talk about something else.

I get the distinct feeling he doesn't want to go further down that road. I choose not to pressure him, in fear of having the conversation grind to a halt. The previous year, in 1998, Skår had exchanged his post as Chairman for that of Managing Director of the Norwegian Space Centre, and had therefore naturally followed the construction of Svalsat at close quarters.

Landsat 1 was launched from Vandenberg Air Force Base in California in July 1972, and Landsat satellites have for the past (almost) 40 years captured millions of images of the Earth.[37] The satellite programme has developed increasingly advanced satellites, and no other satellite systems can match this for time spent capturing Earth images. Naturally the data is also important for the military.

In the seventies and eighties the Pentagon employed Landsat data to make different kinds of maps, and otherwise in connection with the general plan for a possible nuclear war, the SIOP plan. The Pentagon was also quick off the mark in 1989 in offering financial support when the private company Eosat, which owned the satellites, was on the brink of bankruptcy.[38] Nonetheless

---

[37] http://landsat.gsfc.nasa.gov/about/landsat1.html

[38] "U.S Halts Plan to Turn Off the Landsat Satellites", *The New York Times*, 17th March 1989.

it was the invasion of Kuwait two years later that really demonstrated the military value of satellites.

Before the war the maps of Kuwait, Iraq and Saudi-Arabia were old and of inferior quality. For example, the maps that were available for Kuwait were between 10 and 30 years old. In August the year prior to the invasion Landsat 5 began capturing images of the region on commission from the U.S. Defense Forces. The Pentagon purchased images for millions of dollars from the then privately owned American Landsat and the French Spot satellites. The images provided the ordinance survey unit in the U.S. Defense Forces with the opportunity to prepare completely new maps tailor-made for warfare.

A couple of examples: Charts were made showing calculations for water depth down to 50 meters, which was useful for military landings. Charts were also made that showed where vehicles had driven immediately before, on the basis of imprints on grass or sand, information that ground forces on the move would naturally find useful.[39]

The maps numbered 4500 in total, all constantly updated during the war. The number of copies dealt out to the invasion forces totaled a staggering 35 million, all produced with the aid of raw data from Landsat and Spot. Official U.S. documents also state that the coalition forces employed satellite data from Landsat and Spot direct to assess the effect of bomb impacts, monitor Iraqi troop movements and to plan own attacks.

It comes perhaps as no surprise that the U.S. Congress' final report mentions that Landsat and Spot "ensured direct support to the war operations [...] because the satellites provided the military planners with information not normally available [...] and also showed features of the earth beyond human visual detection capability".

Due to the enormous significance Landsat had for the Gulf War, the Pentagon and NASA teamed up to build the next Landsat satellite, Landsat 7. Technical preparations that will make the

---

[39] http://www.gwu.edu/~nsarchiv/NSAEBB/NSAEBB39/, document 10

satellite "even better equipped to be an effective tactical military system in a future conflict", according to a U.S. military rapport.[40] Sometime later the White House issues a press release stating that the Department of Defense is to withdraw from the project's management, but the Pentagon would still be injecting millions of dollars.[41] The press release states 'in black and white' that Landsat has been important for the U.S. Armed Forces for 20 years, and is still important for U.S. security policy.

The situation now is that the latest 'offspring' in the Landsat family, Landsat 7, is increasingly controlled from and downloads data to Svalbard. The same also applies to Landsat 5 – which played such a crucial role during the liberation of Kuwait.[42] From the time Svalsat was established, Landsat has been employed in at any rate in three military operations:

During the war in Kosovo in 1999 NATO forces utilized Landsat to create two and three-dimensional images for planning of air and ground operations, in addition to preparing different types of maps.[43]

Two years later, the war breaks out in Afghanistan, and the Americans employ Landsat for everything from planning and training of operations to assessments of effects of bomb attacks, and to facilitate making airborne drops of emergency aid supplies. Before actual attacks U.S. pilots can use a simulator with 3-dimensional images of the terrain they are to fly over, thus gaining a major advantage in areas that are often impenetrable to most forms of ground or air-based surveillance.[44]

---

[40] http://cryptome.org/jya/sh/sh3.htm

[41] http://www.fas.org/spp/military/docops/national/cnvrgft2.htm

[42] Bo Andersen, "Med rommet som plattform – Med øye for Jorda og den tredje dimensjon", (With space as the platform – and an eye on Earth and the Third Dimension) Norsk Romsenter

[43] http://www.highbeam.com/doc/1G1-54539054.html (registration required to read the complete article)

[44]

Similarly in the U.S. invasion of Iraq in 2003 the Americans utilized images from Landsat "to back up planning/training and gathering of intelligence for operations with fighter and bomber aircraft and to support the ordinance survey units of the Army and Navy", as it is known in military-technical jargon.

A standard formulation in all Norwegian State Budgets from the time Svalsat was established in 1999 up until the present day, is that "Svalsat downloads data for civilian objectives from satellites in Polar orbits and also controls these". The Russians do not believe this statement, even though they have heard it on repeated occasions.

Second in command for the Russian Northern Fleet, Vice Admiral M.V. Motsak, tabled strong arguments against the Norwegian Svalbard policy in a contribution to the Russian military periodical *Military Reflections* in November 2000. He claimed in his article that the satellite plant and other new installations on Svalbard are used for both civilian and military purposes. According to Motsak, Russia must, for these and other reasons than the aforementioned, implement measures to safeguard their interests in the area.[45]

He receives an elaborate reply from the Norwegian ambassador to Russia, Øyvind Nordsletten, in the same periodical one year later, which indicates the Ministry of Foreign Affairs does not regard the initiative from Motsak as a solo initiative, but as an expression for official Russian attitudes.[46] Nordsletten states categorically that Svalsat is engaged exclusively in civilian scientific activity, and that neither Norwegian nor other countries' military authorities are involved in the activity. There is reason to note both of the Norwegian Ambassador's claims.

---

http://www.afcea.org/signal/articles/templates/SIGNAL_Article_Template.asp?articleid=298&zoneid=84
[45] http://dlib.eastview.com/browse/doc/400080
[46] http://dlib.eastview.com/browse/doc/400200

I look at Rolf Skår who is sitting opposite me at the café table. Sure enough, he confirms he knows the Russians weren't happy about the new station: "The Russians made a number of absurd comments. They thought it was a radar and not a satellite station", he says, while shifting uncomfortably in his seat.

Skår is more concerned with filling me in on how Svalsat has expanded. The 71-year old is proud of that he in his time at the Norwegian Space Centre built from the ground up comprehensive space-related activities that had many shaking their heads in disbelief. An activity that provided jobs in Longyearbyen when there was less to do in the mines, and which also ensured justification of the Norwegian Space Centre. Skår is primarily a scientist and an industrial entrepreneur.

"The first agreement with NASA wasn't sufficient. To be able to justify the construction of a permanent station building we had to have more customers. We worked long and hard with the Indian space travel organization ISRO, but that fell through," says Skår.

Kongsberg Gruppen and the American arms manufacturer Lockheed Martin proved to be the saving grace. The companies team up to erect the second antenna by Svalsat. Lockheed Martin is included in return from the American side as part of an agreement on Norwegian purchasing of military equipment in the United States – a so-called repurchase agreement. With that the Ministry of Trade and Commerce allocates funds to a permanent station building.

Lockheed Martin is one of the giants of the American arms industry, and together with Kongsberg Gruppen had plans to make Svalbard into a world-leading satellite station. The project is not a success, and after a short period Lockheed Martin pulls completely out of Svalbard. Skår is not willing to say anything about the background for this move, but it is obvious there were satellites at that time with even more obvious military purposes that wished to use Svalbard. There is reason to ask whether the

Svalbard Treaty was considered too difficult a hurdle for Lockheed Martin to deal with.

In the first few years after the turn of the millennium the situation is such that Svalsat is established as a ground station with the world's best site for Polar-orbiting satellites. The majority of earth observation satellites travel in a Polar orbit, and the number of satellites is increasing significantly. Nonetheless, competition is extremely keen.

The American companies Northrop Grumman and Raytheon are commissioned by U.S. civilian and military authorities to establish a whole new generation of environmental and weather satellites. To Skår's great disappointment the companies choose Helsinki rather than Svalbard as a ground station. The reason is that Helsinki, as opposed to Svalbard, has good fiber links to the United States, which ensures cheaper and safer transport of data.

Skår now pulls out all the stops so that Svalbard and not Helsinki will draw the longest straw when the U.S. authorities make the final decision. This means that Svalbard must also be equipped with fiber.

In the year 2000 Norway and the United States entered into a mutual formal agreement to develop space co-operation. Skår uses this agreement for all it's worth, and takes advantage of any and all personal friendships and acquaintances in politics and industry on both sides of the Atlantic, built up ever since the first plans for Svalsat saw light in 1995. This is one fight he is determined to win.

Washington 31st October 2002. Skår readies himself for a string of meetings that will determine Svalsat's future. Norway wants the United States to pay for a fiber cable, but there is no money in the U.S. budget for this. In the afternoon Skår has a private meeting with John D. Cunningham, top executive for the Integrated Program Office (IPO). The IPO is a collaboration between the Pentagon, the American Chamber of Commerce and NASA to develop the next generation of environmental and weather satellites, the National Polar-orbiting Operational Environmental Satellite System, (NPOESS).

Skår suggests the amount the United States must spend with continued transfer of data from Svalbard via commercial communication satellites in the space of three-four years, is allocated instead to finance a fiber cable to the mainland, and that the United States then gets to use the cable more or less free for 25 years thereafter. Cunningham finds this proposal very attractive. His first choice is Svalbard, and he promises to do what he can to achieve the proposed financial solution.[47]

Skår employs every trick in the book. He invites the Americans to Svalbard, takes them on a scooter safari to the Russian settlement of Barentsburg, and serves up the best there is on the menu from the exclusive restaurant *Huset* in Longyearbyen. The enthusiastic director also enlists the support of the Minister of Trade and Industry Ansgar Gabrielsen. Gabrielsen backs the financial solution and writes letters to several relevant U.S. authorities.[48]

In the end Skår gets his way: An agreement is prepared. Outwardly this is presented as a breakthrough for the civilian American weather report service's and NASA's use of Svalsat. Not a word is mentioned about the new opportunities now afforded the Pentagon. The U.S. Armed Forces inject 25 million dollars, or one-third of the total cost. It goes without saying the Pentagon wants something in return.

It's the summer of 2003 and two of the world's most advanced specialist fiber cable laying vessels are anchored off Longyearbyen and Harstad. On 21st July "Maersk Recorder" begins stretching fiber cable southwards from Hotellneset on Svalbard. Five days later "Cable Innovator" commences with the same operation from Breivika near Harstad but in a northward

---

[47] http://www.telektronikk.com/volumes/pdf/3.2004/Page_134-139.pdf
[48] Letter of support on financing 19.05.03, with references to three similar letters

direction. The vessels meet out at sea, and the cables are spliced. The vessels then lay a new cable in another route in the same way. Svalbard then has two independent fiber connections, which leaves data traffic less vulnerable to technical faults or military attack. Never before has cable been laid in the sea at depths below 1000 meters, but everything proceeds according to plan. The cables are instrumental in the establishment of Svalbard as a global communication center.

'The Cable Chief' – as the Minister of Trade and Commerce Ansgar Gabrielsen calls Skår at the official opening in Longyearbyen January 2004 – is satisfied. Svalsat becomes the ground station for the next generation of civilian and military U.S. environmental and weather satellites, NPOESS, which among other things will contribute with information enabling better decisions in tactical military operations to be made.

The Americans are also thrilled with the financial solution. A report from a research institution under the auspices of the U.S. Navy concludes the agreement will save U.S. taxpayers 140 million dollars in the course of a 20-year period.[49]

In addition to that Svalsat has the world's best site for Polar-orbiting satellites Svalsat can, thanks to the new fiber cable, now also offer new customers cheaper transport of data from the ground station to places across the globe than competing ground stations. Soon satellite companies from all over the world are queuing up to utilize Svalbard – this also applies to satellites with distinct military objectives. One example is the Italian COSMO-SkyMed, which has received permission from the Norwegian Post and Telecommunications Authority to use Svalsat. The permit openly acknowledges that the satellite system for earth observation will have military users.[50]

---

[49]

http://edocs.nps.edu/npspubs/scholarly/MBAPR/2006/Jun/06Jun_Buchanan_MBA.pdf

[50] Permit for COSMO-SkyMed satellites, 09.12.09

Once again Rolf Skår has created a Norwegian industrial success story. At Kokos café in Lillestrøm I am also aware that he already many years ago knew parts of the operation of Svalsat presented a problem in relation to the Svalbard Treaty. In an interview with the specialist journal Space News in March 2004 Skår is asked whether military observation satellites are a market for Svalsat, to which he replies: " This remains a sensitive issue, in part of the Svalbard Treaty, which limits the island to peaceful activities. Satellites are dual-use by their nature, but how far we can go in this area is not clear."[51]

I don't want to confront Skår at this moment with the contents of his interview with Space News. Skår has already several times stated categorically that questions in relation to the treaty are the responsibility of the authorities'. It also strikes me amiable contact with Skår could prove very helpful in completing the book. On our way out from the café, Skår suddenly says: "I could have refused to talk to you when you rang me yesterday. And I could have said no to meet you today. But I decided to meet you so that you would get the most correct possible image of how everything took place. I know why you have so many questions. I've checked you out on Google and saw you were awarded Tore Sandberg's investigative journalism grant", says Skår, with just a hint of a smile that negates any effort of mine to interpret.

Eventually the Norwegian Post and Telecommunications Authority grows increasingly skeptical about the staggering rate at which the satellite station is developing on Svalbard. Possibly Skår has also long known that one day a difficult public debate would rear its head regarding satellite activity on Svalbard. Perhaps it's the case that he took the decision some time ago that the best way to meet that debate would be to go on the offensive.

---

[51] "Picking the best tools for the job", Space News, 16 mars 2004

Chapter 5
"A hellish problem"

Charming old white-painted timber cottages gathered in a tight cluster around a sheltered cove, interconnected by a network of narrow alleys and roads. I am in Lillesand, as far away as it is possible to be from Svalbard in Norway. But nonetheless it is here the decision is made on which satellites can use Svalbard. In an imposing building of steel and glass, squeezed between modest wooden buildings, is where the Norwegian Post and Telecommunications Authority (NPT) has its headquarters.

Director Geir Jan Sundal receives me in a tidy corner office on the second floor with glass walls looking out towards the Southern Norwegian town. Sundal is a sturdy-built chap with a long history in this branch of industry.

The Director had gone out of his way to arrange a suitable time for us to meet, and he gave the impression he was interested in the issues I raised when I rang him. Sundal has no problem admitting he thinks the handling of applications for satellite activity permits on Svalbard, is difficult. He grins ever so slightly when he replies: "All this rigmarole about who does what and who has authority and responsibility for this, that and the other, is a little tricky you could say. There simply is no miracle solution. It was possibly more appropriate in the old days; but in any case it certainly hasn't become any easier with all the new technology there is in space and on the ground," said Sundal.

The NPT is responsible for handling the applications, but has no own technical and judicial competence in relation to assessing applications up against the Svalbard Treaty's provisions that prevent use of the archipelago for warlike purposes. Initially, the NPT sends the individual applications to the Norwegian Defense Research Establishment (NDRE), for a technical-military evaluation. From there the applications are sent together with the evaluations from the NDRE to the Ministry of Foreign Affairs, the Ministry of Justice and the Governor for judicial evaluation before the final decision is made. According to Sundal it has been difficult to obtain clear guidelines from the Ministry of Foreign Affairs:

"We've always had problems with getting the relevant authorities to give a clear yes or no to new satellites. In the end, we are the ones who issue the permit, no problem with that. But that decision is based on approval by the Ministry of Foreign Affairs, the Ministry of Justice and the Governor. Naturally, when it takes a while to get a reply from them, and you have Svalsat knocking at the door asking why they haven't received a permit, life tends to get complicated," said Sundal, who also admits they are under a certain amount of pressure from the Ministry of Trade and Commerce in relation to new industrial activity.

"Has this in a way forced you to engage in foreign politics?"

"Yes, or to be precise, we have at times felt that if we are to get anywhere with this, we have to just cut through the semantics because we've not been given any clear answer," says Sundal, adding that the rapid development of technology is a further problem in that this has produced several new generations of satellites since the NPT requested a new, clearer set of regulations.

Deputy Director General Jørn Ringlund of the Ministry of Transport and Communications has confirmed previously that the ministry has worked on a new set of regulations, but declines to say anything about when they will be ready because – as he said – "the matter is under internal consideration", which it has been - since 2002.[52]

Consideration for the Svalbard Treaty has concerned the authorities to a greater or lesser extent since the tentative early

---

[52] Annual Report Post- og teletilsynet 2002 (The Norwegian Post and Telecommunications Authority)

stages for satellite activity on Svalbard. The Norwegian Space Centre's Annual Report for 1996 states the following:

"Activity on Svalbard complies with the guidelines as stated in the terms of the Svalbard Treaty. Both Svalsat and Svalrak [missile launch station] have been assessed in relation to this and Government approval has been given."

This takes place after a comprehensive process between several ministries, the Norwegian Space Centre and the Governor of Svalbard. The Norwegian Space Centre presents documentation showing that all activity will be exclusively scientific and civilian, and the matter is circulated for extensive comment. On the Norwegian side there is sympathy for the Russian skepticism about Norwegian satellite plans. In the mid-nineties there is a political thaw in relations between east and west without which it had not been possible to establish a satellite station.[53]

The (former) Soviet Union and later Russia have always maintained that the Svalbard Treaty's requirements in the original language of French on "l'utilisation pacifique" – peaceful utilisation - and the prohibition of plant/installations intended for warlike purposes – "devront jamais être utilisées dans un but de guerre", means a total ban on military activity on the archipelago. Russia maintains Svalbard shall be a demilitarized area.[54]

Norway, for its part, has always practiced a restrictive interpretation of the treaty in relation to military activity. This is apparent in for example the Parliamentary Report number 9 from 1999. There it is stressed that the airport at Svalbard shall only be in use for civil aviation purposes, which is also stipulated in a written agreement between Norway and Russia. This led to military transport aircraft being denied permission to land on

---

[53] Based on amongst sources statements by Pål Sørensen, previously Managing Director of Norsk Romsenter (The Norwegian Space Centre)
[54] Conversation with the Russian Ambassador Sergey Vadimovich Andreev in Oslo

Svalbard up until 2010, even when this has for example only concerned transport of civilian research expeditions.

The authorities realized it was necessary to prepare a set of regulations that ensured that new satellite activity would not breach the Svalbard Treaty. The Ministry of Transport already had regulations in place governing satellite activity for mainland Norway. The NPT is responsible for granting permits and otherwise for enforcing the said regulations. A new chapter was added to the regulations to ensure ground stations on Svalbard do not breach the Svalbard Treaty.[55]

The NPT is responsible for granting permits, even though it is primarily the State that concerns itself with the administration of frequencies and has neither military nor Treaty-judicial competence.[56] The NPT was skeptical toward the arrangement already when it was circulated for comment. The Governor has the formal responsibility for keeping check on the satellite activity, an activity that is at the absolute leading edge of advanced technology. The current situation is such that the Governor still doesn't have own technical expertise at his disposal. The inspection task is carried out by a lawyer, who dedicates 50 % of his full time position to the work.[57]

The new regulations come into force on 11th June 1999. Two years have passed since Svalsat, downloaded satellite signals for the first time and two months after Svalsat commenced its first normal satellite operation. As we have already seen, the first satellite, Landsat 7, is employed to assess the effect of bombing attacks and other aspects of warfare.

---

[55] http://www.lovdata.no/cgi-wift/wiftldles?doc=/app/gratis/www/docroot/for/sf/sd/sd-19990611-0664.html&emne=jordstasjon*%20for*%20satellitt*&
[56] Conversations with representatives for Post- og teletilsynet (The Norwegian Post and Telecommunications Authority)

[57] Conversation with Assistant Governor Lars Fause, November 2010

In the autumn of 2000 the Governor carries out the first two inspections of Svalsat.[58] The regulation provides the Governor with the opportunity to employ the expertise of Richard B. Olsen from the Norwegian Defense Research Establishment NDRE and Stein Gudbjørgsrud from the NPT also participate. The NPT examines whether the satellites have communicated with the satellites they have permission for, and concludes that the satellites cannot be connected to military purposes and that the activity is conducted in accordance with the treaty.

The group is nonetheless critical that they are not allowed insight into the kind of data that is actually downloaded, and contend that the authorities should assess whether the data sent from the station should be reportable. To date, no action has been taken. To this very day the NPT still does not have insight into the content of data sent from Svalbard.[59]

Only three short years after the new regulations for Svalbard came into force patience has worn very thin at the NPT. The inspectorate's annual report for 2002 states:

> It is recommended that the regulation for the satellite ground station should be updated – out of consideration to changes in both the Telecommunications Act (later the Electronic Communications Act) and to the need for inspection of other types of radio station on Svalbard. A new generation of satellites is appearing that often contain both civilian and military components, at the same time as the accuracy of the data is much improved. This may imply a source of conflict with the way applications are currently dealt with in regard to the Svalbard Treaty. The NDRE will prepare a document describing possible approaches to the problems that can be used as the basis for decision-making by the ministries and departments that are involved in this work.

---

[58] Minutes of inspection at Svalsat, 11th October 2000
[59] Conversation with Assistant Governor Lars Fause, November 2010

Translator's note: (The Electronic Communications Act came into force on July 25 2003 and replaced the Telecommunications Act 1995)

What happened to this work? Was a document prepared by the NDRE I ask the Deputy Director General of the NPT, who turned a light shade of embarrassed pink. "A report was prepared that took much longer time than planned. The report is no doubt out to hearing and comments now. This is a matter for the Polar Committee, a panel of representatives from the ministries of Foreign Affairs, Justice and Transport and Communications. We are not included there. We are still waiting. We can push and push, but we can't force anything to happen. We can only raise the subject at regular intervals," said a somewhat dejected Sundal.

The annual report for the NPT the following year in 2003 states the department is truly anxious about developments:

A new generation of satellites has now emerged with improved technical efficiency in regard to both optical and other instruments for observation of the earth's surface. Data from these instruments can be utilized for military applications. [...] Several satellites are now so-called "dual-use", where both civilian and military payloads are placed on board the satellite. In reality, it would prove impracticable to check which administrative guidelines apply to civilian customers and which ones apply to military. Satellite activities in a number of countries, including the United States, have been reorganized in recent years. In the United States civilian and military meteorological services now use the same satellites and the same data. [...] A fiber cable has been laid from Svalbard to the mainland that enables huge volumes of raw data to be transported swiftly to the receiver. Three of the last four applications from the Norwegian Space Centre deal with activity as described overhead. A restrictive interpretation of the Svalbard Treaty would imply that these applications must be declined. A robust interpretation of the treaty would imply that the applications can be approved, in which case the inspection would likely be more exacting (in order for the Norwegian authorities to retain credibility in regard to other states.) A restrictive interpretation further implies that the Norwegian Space Centre would encounter major problems when competing for new contracts. The advantage here would be a subsequent avoidance of difficult political situations.

In this period there are many meetings between the NPT, the Governor of Svalbard, the Ministry of Justice and the Ministry of Foreign Affairs. The NPT are not satisfied with the answers they are given as they lack clear definition. Once again the inspectorate has the feeling they have been left holding the baby.

It ends up with the NPT concluding a year later that "it is no longer desirable or actual to prohibit communication with satellites that potentially can be utilized for military purposes." The NPT's annual report for 2004 also states that "such an interpretation of the regulations and (political) objectives would be that the authorities [...] must carry out inspections [...] on Svalbard to monitor usage with regard to compliance with the terms of the Svalbard Treaty."

Nonetheless there is still no inspection of the content of large volume of data generated at Svalbard, the only check being that the satellite station communicates with the satellites for which permits have been granted. There is now a veritable rainstorm of permits. Amongst the most interesting are Kompsat-2, Formosat-2, Radarsat-1 and the American Defense Meteorological (DMSP), (NPP) and (NPOESS) satellites. We'll take a closer look at these.

The U.S. military meteorological forecasting service, DMSP, has existed since the early sixties. Now there are always at least two DMSP satellites operative in a Polar orbit that update weather and environmental data for the entire planet in a 14-hour period, also for areas where the United States for political reasons is denied access. The most important instrument is the Operational Linescan System, which continually scans cloud bases over wide expanses.

Satellites are also crucial for military activity in space.[60] Radiation from the sun varies and affects radar plant capability to warn of nuclear attack and other radar systems. DMSP measures these changes. DMSP measures various factors that in total enable correct weather observations and weather forecasts for outer space.[61] This is vital for everything from secure satellite communication to being able to detect hostile satellites. The United States currently has at least 104 active military satellites.

NPT officials handling applications are perplexed and don't quite know what to do when DMSP applies to use Svalbard. The application is being processed at the same time the NPT finds there is now a tacit political acceptance for changing the policy concerning allocation. Previously only exclusively civilian satellites were approved. Now certain military objectives are accepted. Where then is the line drawn?

It doesn't get any easier when the United States decides to merge the military and civilian weather and environmental forecasting service. Operation of the DMSP satellites is transferred to the civilian U.S. meteorological service, but it is still the U.S. Air Force that pays for "DMSP continuing to ensure the gathering of precise, reliable global environmental data as a support factor in warfare".[62]

To complicate things even further; the significance of a permit granted to DMSP is extremely important for Svalsat's ambitions to become the world's biggest ground station for Polar-orbiting satellites. The largest shareholder in Svalsat is the Ministry of Trade and Commerce. The ministry contributed to the financing of the laying of fiber cables between Svalbard and the mainland. The competition to become the ground station for civilian/military U.S. weather and environmental data services was

---

[60] http://www.defenseindustrydaily.com/DMSP-Tempest-Tracker-for-the-US-Military-06140/

[61] http://www.eoportal.org/directory/pres_NPOESSNationalPolarorbitingOperatio nalEnvironmentalSatelliteSystem.html

[62] http://www.af.mil/information/factsheets/factsheet_print.asp?fsID=94&page=1

extreme, and threatened Svalsat's development potential, a contest that resulted in Norway and the United States teaming up to lay a fiber cable to the mainland. Now that the cable is laid, the United States is eager to establish Svalbard as the principal ground station to control the new generation of U.S. civilian/military weather and environmental satellites, NPOESS.[63] DMSP must nonetheless continue to function during a long transition period, and the Americans wish to use Svalbard for all its weather and environmental satellites.

Under Secretary of the Air Force and Pentagon space czar Peter B. Teets, said in 2003 that "the nation's unparalleled ability to exploit weather and environmental data gathered from space is critical to the success of military operations". With the new generation of weather and environmental satellites the focus is changing from "dealing with the weather" to utilizing data on the atmosphere and conditions in outer space directly in warfare. One reason is that the time from observation until the information arrives at battlefield level is cut down from hours to minutes, whether this applies to sea, land or outer space.

In 2005 the NPT granted permits to the six DMSP satellites, the civilian American meteorological satellites, an experimental satellite for the new military/civilian American weather and environmental data satellites and for the planned fleet of new weather and environmental data satellites NPOESS.

The following was written by one of the two principal contractors for NPOESS, the American company Raytheon, on amongst other things the military's use of the new system:

NPOESS data on ground humidity will ensure safe, secure and rapid troop movements. Precise measurements of ambient humidity and temperature will increase the efficiency and effectiveness of the artillery. Precise

---

[63]

http://www.ipo.noaa.gov/IPOarchive/ED/Articles/AIAA_2008_NPOESS_Manu script_135280_final.pdf measurements of wind at sea level will enable fighter aircraft to take off from, return to and man oeuvre with vastly improved safety margins and to have greatly increased impact. […] Improved weather data from NPOESS will change the manner in which the military utilizes knowledge of the environment in warfare. Precision weapons, precise maneuvering and precise timing will all be improved, and this in time will provide our troops and forces with advantages over the enemy who do not have access to detailed knowledge of when and how the weather will change.

Svalsat has long since been engaged in a 'preliminary' co-operation with the American group Raytheon on NPOESS. As early as in 2004 Svalsat received an award for its work. March 23, Rolf Skatteboe, director of Svalsat's parent company, Kongsberg Satellite Services, was at Raytheon's headquarters in Colorado where he received US$ 50 000 and a crystal trophy for his efforts in building up the new system.

Development of technology and other pilot projects for NPOESS proceed as normal, but President Barack Obama has split the main project into a civilian and a military section. The reason is understood to be that the Pentagon is unable to reach agreement with the civilian faction. Work with the experimental satellite progresses at a steady rate, and providing all goes according to plan it will be launched in 2011. Separate antenna systems have been built on Svalbard.[64]

Meanwhile the old U.S. military and civilian weather and environmental data satellites continue their 14 earth orbits every 24-hours. As soon as they appear over the horizon and are able to communicate with Svalsat, they dump data regardless of whether this is from Pakistan, Afghanistan or from outer space.

---

[64] http://www.ipo.noaa.gov/IPOarchive/ED/Articles/AIAA_2008_NPOESS_Manu script_135280_final.pdf

The second satellite system we will examine is Radarsat. Originally Radarsat was the result of a request from Canadian authorities for better earth observation for civilian and military purposes of the world's second largest country, in particular its northern reaches.

On 4th November 1999 Radarsat-1 was launched from Vandenberg Air Force Base in a Polar orbit. This earth observation satellite is special in that it produces images using radio signals reflected from the ground and re-captured by the satellite. This is a different technology than that used by satellites that capture images with a camera. Radarsat-1 can, as opposed to earth observation satellites with cameras, also produce images through clouds and in darkness. This is of enormous interest to the military.

From Day One the U.S. military intelligence services and other military departments are major customers of Radarsat data.[65] The Americans enter into a number of contracts in connection with military operations in both Afghanistan and Iraq.[66] Open NATO documents relate how intelligence services use Radarsat-1 in Iraq to plan how best to move military equipment in and out of the airport in Baghdad, and to ascertain the level of damage inflicted by the Iraqi forces on its own storage facilities and military equipment before fleeing.[67] The U.S. Army is particularly pleased they are able to download satellite data from Radarsat and other satellites directly to the combat zones for planning missions, exercises and intelligence purposes.

The Norwegian Armed Forces also put Radarsat-1 to use. Already a year after it is launched from California, satellite data is ticking in about the Barents Sea and North Sea via Kongsberg Satellite Services' receiver station in Tromsø to the Norwegian Armed Forces interpretation center at Fauske, which is a part of the Norwegian intelligence service.[68] Here the data is analyzed before

---

[65] http://www.canada.com/topics/news/national/story.html?id=3355b03f-aaa7-4f01-83d6-0304bde28d45
[66] http://www.disam.dsca.mil/pubs/v.23_4/hartmetz.pdf
[67] http://www.disam.dsca.mil/pubs/v.23_4/hartmetz.pdf

being sent on to Regional Command North Norway's joint operation room, the Norwegian Coastguard and Andøya airbase. The airbase uses radar images in planning new sorties with its Orion surveillance aircraft. The Joint Operations Headquarters and the FFI/NDRE also receive the radar images.

The data can be read directly into the operative command and control systems. The FFI/NDRE used, among others, the data during the NATO exercise Strong Resolve off the Møre coast in 2002, to detect hostile vessels and for information about sea fronts and other meteorological conditions for use in planning of operations.[69] The Norwegian Armed Forces order and purchase data from Radarsat-1 for several million annually, in 2005 the bill was in the region of NOK 5 million.

The Norwegian Armed Forces are delighted with the Radarsat-1 co-operation, and a mutual co-operation agreement is entered into between Norway and Canada. Norway eventually buys into the owner side of the satellite system.[70] But the receiver station in Tromsø can only download satellite data for Radarsat-1 for 12 of the 14 times the satellite orbits the earth every twenty-four hours. This contrasts with Svalsat, which can receive signals from all the orbits, as the station lies closer to the North Pole. Kongsberg Satellite Services therefore campaigns to have the station at Svalbard also download data from Radarsat-1.

The NPT follows normal routines and sends the matter to the FFI/NDRE for an expert evaluation of whether Radarsat-1 can be used in warfare, and thus is in conflict with the terms of the Svalbard Treaty. In that there are such close ties between the Norwegian Armed Forces and Radarsat it should perhaps come as

---

[68] http://www.regjeringen.no/nb/dep/jd/dok/nouer/2000/nou-2000-24/10/2.html?id=361108

[69] From Norwegian Defense Research Establishment history, "Satellite surveillance", March 2003

[70] See http://www.spaceref.com/news/viewpr.html?pid=10933 and *The Annual Report from Norsk Romsenter, (The Norwegian Space Centre)* 2007

no surprise that Radarsat-1 receives a permit to be controlled from and have data downloaded on Svalbard.[71]

The Parliamentary Control Committee for intelligence, surveillance and security services has now taken an interest in Svalsat in connection with Norway's commitments in the Svalbard Treaty. 22 April 2004 the panel was on Svalbard where they were briefed by the Governor. The panel followed up this matter at a meeting with the Norwegian Intelligence Service (NIS), where it was claimed the service had neither operational, financial nor any other associations with the Svalbard Satellite station. Data from Radarsat has for many years now been analyzed by the NIS Interpretation Centre at Fauske for further use by the Norwegian Armed Forces.

Back to Director Geir Jan Sundal's corner office at NPT headquarters in Lillesand. I ask if he remembers the handling of Radarsat-1's application and knows of the Armed Forces' use of this satellite, to which he replies: "No, unfortunately I don't."

I get the impression Sundal is more than a little embarrassed. However it is important to remember that in total there are now more than a hundred satellites with permits to use Svalbard. I note that Sundal doesn't ask me about my knowledge regarding the link between military interests and Radarsat.

We have seen that Svalsat and Kongsberg Satellite Services (KSAT) have worked actively towards Canada and the United States. But KSAT has ambitions to make Svalsat a world-leading ground station for Polar-orbiting satellites, with customers across the globe. Interest is considerable due to Svalsat's favourable geographical position and good communications. In fact it is only Russia that doesn't need to use Svalbard, as that country, with its ground stations from the Kola Peninsula in the west to the Kamtsjatka Peninsula in the east, can communicate with Polar satellites during all their orbits.

---

[71] Permit to download data from Radarsat-1 to Svalsat given in Letter of Permit, 16.01.06

64

Taiwan is one of the many countries to show interest for Svalbard. Even though in reality Taiwan has existed as an independent state for more than 50 years, China still maintains that Taiwan is part of China, and sparks still fly on occasions between the two countries. In 1996–1997 China conducted a number of major military exercises in the Taiwan Strait that separates China and Taiwan, while the United States shows its support for Taiwan by sending a fleet of aircraft carriers. A crass war of words ensues with China threatening to invade.

As late as 2005 the People's Congress in Beijing passes a new law that would allow an attack on Taiwan in the event of a formal severance from China, and then sites around 500 short and medium range missiles in the Fujian district by the Taiwan Strait, all of which are aimed in the direction of Taiwan.

This is the reason why Taiwan sets in massive resources in order to meet China on a military level, but also to develop its own satellite technology. Formosat-2 is launched from Vandenberg Air Force Base on 21st May 2004. It weighs 742 kilos, is 2.4 meters tall and has a radius of 1.6 meters. The satellite is an earth observation satellite with a resolution of two meters, and is immediately launched into a Polar orbit.

The satellite is programmed and controlled to capture images of selected areas of Taiwan and surrounding areas once every 24-hours, a frequency other satellites are not capable of. The most important task is to take high-resolution images of the Chinese mainland, especially the coastal areas facing Taiwan, from where any attack is expected to originate.[72]

The satellite can also capture images from any global location in that it is a Polar satellite. This capacity is utilized by the commercial European company SPOT, which negotiates an agreement with the Taiwanese authorities to be the exclusive

---

[72] http://www.geoinformatics.com/blog/online-articles/space-image-acquisition-for-geospatial-intelligence (Formosat-2 is called Rocsat-2 here)

receiver and forwarding sales channel for all data from Formosat-2, with the exception of Taiwan and China.[73]

SPOT goes public and markets data from Formosat-2 to potential military customers around the globe. There is reason to note that Formosat-2 is first and foremost marketed for military purposes, to a lesser degree for civilian purposes, such as keeping up with development of terrestrial and forestry industry growth, and to make better civilian maps. Here is an excerpt from a presentation of the satellite that the head of the business division of SPOT IMAGE, Sayag Daniel, gave during an international conference held in Sofia, Bulgaria, during the winter of 2007:

> Ideally suited to strategic and operational intelligence missions, it is able to identify and characterize military sites, naval bases, air bases and refugee camps; perform reconnaissance of ships, aircraft and other assets; and surveillance of strategic or industrial facilities.[74]

The websites for SPOT and SPOT's subsidiaries offer a great deal of information about Formosat-2. It appears the company uses data from Formosat-2 together with data from other satellites to make 3-dimensional images with an accuracy of 10 meters vertically and 15 meters horizontally. The 3-dimensional images are used to plan and evaluate operations against hostile threats, to identify targets and exact positions of targets as well as assess the scope of damage after an attack. Formosat-2 communicates with SPOT's geographic reference system, Referense3D, which has an agreement with the U.S. military intelligence service NGA, and is accurate enough to input databases into missiles and piloted and unmanned aircraft.[75]

---

[73] See previous footnote

[74] http://www.rgz.gov.rs/DocF/Files/intergeo-east-2007/n42_a.pdf

[75] http://www.spot.com/web/SICORP/1750-spot-image-provides-dem-data-to-the-nga-for-global-foundation-database.php

Furthermore, SPOT, with its knowledge of and access to satellite data has also participated in establishing intelligence centers in several countries, so that these countries' armed forces have gained their own independent intelligence information.[76] SPOT does not publicize information concerning the identity of these countries.

In 2005 Norwegian Space Centre receives a permit from the NPT to control and give commands, and download data for Formosat-2 at Svalsat. Data downloaded from Formosat-2 at Svalsat is sent to customers all over the world via the new fiber cable in a matter of milliseconds.

The Minister of Foreign Affairs Jonas Gahr Støre wrote to Parliament in the winter of 2010: "The Svalbard Treaty stipulates certain specific regulations for the archipelago. The Norwegian authorities have always been focused on ensuring full compliance with the treaty's regulations."

Taiwan isn't the only country in Asia at odds with its neighbor. Relations between South Korea and North Korea are not of the best. As is the case with the conflict between Taiwan and China, the conflict between South Korea and North Korea has existed for decades. The background lies in the establishment of the two countries. The two victors after World War II, the United States and Russia could not agree who should lead a government for the entire Korean peninsula, which after the war lead to the formation of South and North Korea. Since then the two states have been like cat and dog, each side often supported by major powers.

One of the most serious incidents occurred on 20th May 2010, when a North Korean submarine torpedoed the South Korean naval vessel 'Cheonan'. The corvette broke in two and sank, taking with it its crew of 46. In the immediate aftermath there was a real fear that a hot war would break out between the two countries.

---

[76] http://www.spotimage.com/web/en/1803-defence-intelligence-security.php

Just before Christmas the same year things came to a head again. This time there were regular exchanges of fire between soldiers on an island adjacent to the borders of both states, which once more gave cause to fear full-scale war would erupt between the two states, with the consequences this would have.

North Korea has carried out tests with short, medium and long-range missiles. According to the United States the country has enough uranium to produce nuclear weapons. That's quite naturally reason enough for South Korea to want to know what its Northern neighbor is up to.

A few years before the launch, on 17th March 2004, Kongsberg Satellite Services Managing Director, Rolf Skatteboe, is in the city of Taejon in South Korea to sign a contract between Kongsberg Satellite Services and the Korean Space Organisation KARI. Agreement is reached that Svalsat will operate as the ground station for the planned South Korean earth observation satellite Kompsat-2. During the ceremony Skatteboe holds a short speech: "I'm very impressed with the Korean space programme and the future satellite projects for the Korean space authorities. Kongsberg Satellite Services is very proud that the Korean space organization decided on our services for the new project."

Nothing is said about the military significance or about the collision with Norwegian commitments in relation to the Svalbard Treaty. In the application to the NPT, Kongsberg Satellite Services states that the satellite will be used for mapping of natural resources, production of maps and atmospheric research.

On 28th July 2006, 11:05am, the Russian launching vehicle 'Rockot' rises majestically from the rocket launch pad in Plesetsk near Archangel in Northwest Russia, carrying South Korea's first spy satellite. This satellite is also Polar-orbiting, and uses Svalsat as the ground station. Korea Multi-purpose Satellite 2 (Kompsat-2) is South Korea's first earth observation satellite, and is alleged to have double the image resolution quality as Formosat-2. Kompsat-2 is said to be capable of identifying objects with a diameter of one

68

meter, and will capture images of the Korean peninsula three times daily.
9933

The main task is to capture images of nuclear installations and other military plant in North Korea. The images are analyzed by both NIS and KDIA, South Korean intelligence agencies.[77]

Well-reputed researchers and experts agree that Kompsat-2 has major military significance for South Korea. Here is an analysis from Stratfor, which is an international network of intelligence experts:

> Systems such as the Arirang-2 serve more than economic and technological goals or issues of national pride. South Korea has long been "blind" with regard to North Korea, at least as far as satellite imagery is concerned. South Korea's military and intelligence services thus have had to rely on U.S. satellites or purchased commercial imagery. At times, this has created a delay in gathering information, slowing the decision-making process and creating tensions between Seoul and Washington. Arirang-2 adresses this gap, at least in part.

As with Formosat-2, Kompsat-2 captures images of the entire planet, but South Korea only needs photos of Korea. South Korea also negotiates an agreement with SPOT that gives the company exclusive rights to images from all over the world, with the exception of Korea, the Middle East and the United States, which South Korea holds the rights to.[78] South Korea's close political and military ties with the United States has to be the explanation why the Middle East and the United States are excluded.

SPOT, for its part, gets a new, advanced satellite in its portfolio, which is openly marketed as a vital instrument for engaging in modern warfare, alone or in co-operation with

---

[77] See note 72
[78] See note 72

Formosat-2 and other satellites that the company owns or has rights to. Kompsat-2 is marketed as follows on SPOT IMAGE's website:

> Kompsat-2, with its extremely fine resolution is a cornerstone in effective reconnoitering. Ideal for the collection of tactical and strategic intelligence, it supports the identification and characterization of sensitive locations, as well as the reconnoitering and identification of civilian and military systems.

Using Kompsat-2 images with one-meter resolution one can:

> *See*: vehicles, artillery, storage facilities.
> *Approximately identify*: vehicles, nuclear weapons, chemical weapons and biological weapons, radar and communications equipment, rocket launching ramps.
> *Precisely identify*: Ground troops, aircraft, roads, command centers and minefields.
> *Identify*: Submarines, bridges, harbors/ports and harbor/port areas, railway areas and urban areas.

SPOT guarantees that the company, with the help of Kompsat-2, Formosat-2 and other satellites, can capture detailed images from any location on the globe regardless of weather, in daylight and darkness, within a 24-hour period. This, together with access to an image archive of several million images provides the possibility of constructing three-dimensional images and support for military actions that was simply impossible just a few years ago. SPOT makes no attempt to conceal the fact that both Formosat-2 and Kompsat-2 are utilized to plan and implement military operations, whether this be in connection with threat evaluation, target detection and location, and damage assessment.[79]

Until 2007 the French space exploration organization CNES was the majority shareholder in SPOT. Since then it has been Astrium, which is Europe's leading industrial company

---

[79] http://www.spotasia.com.sg/web/sg/2618-defence-intelligence-security.php

concentrated on military and civilian space travel activity with 15 000 employees, which has had the biggest holding. There is thus no reason to doubt the content of the company's website is correct.

I don't mention to NPT's Geir Jan Sundal about my discovery. I want full control of my information for a while yet. Publication of the book is still a long way off. However I do say it's possible to find a lot of information on the Internet about the true functions of satellites that use Svalbard.

We go to the canteen for a bite to eat. I touch on a phone conversation we had prior to our meeting. I remind him that he, after we had agreed to talk without being quoted, had said that the satellite applications were "a hellish problem with an outdated set of regulations". I ask if I can nonetheless quote him on that statement. He says it depends in what context. He later gave his permission. The NPT is not comfortable with having the responsibility of allocating permits on the basis of the current set of regulations.

Chapter 6
Satellites for War

The Norwegian Post and Telecommunications Authority no longer issues permits solely to purely commercial satellites. The Authority is now authorized to issue permits to satellites that have both civil and military objectives. The question that immediately springs to mind is naturally enough which military objectives the Norwegian Post and Telecommunications Authority is permitted to approve while ensuring that satellite activities do not conflict with the Treaty of Svalbard. The Norwegian Post and Telecommunications Authority is in other words authorized to give its approval to satellites that can or will be used for military purposes, but not for "warlike purposes" as laid down in the Treaty of Svalbard.

The owners of the satellites, who submit the applications, are located in all parts of the world, and the Norwegian Post and Telecommunications Authority does not embark on any investigation of the satellites before they go into orbit. The Authority must rely on information supplied by the Norwegian Space Centre, the formal applicant for Svalsat, which organization in turn receives information from its potential customers. This is no easy task. India, a nation experiencing certain problems with one of its neighbors, is one of the countries that wish to avail themselves of Svalsat's services.

In May 1999 India discovers that large military forces from Pakistan have crossed the border between the countries and entered the mountainous areas of Kashmir. A fire-fight breaks out, and the result is the most serious military conflict between Pakistan and India since both nations developed nuclear weapons.[80]

After two months of bitter fighting India has forced the Pakistani forces back over the border. The USA exerts pressure on Pakistan, and the conflict ends. By this time thousands of soldiers

---

[80] http://csis.org/files/media/csis/pubs/sam12.pdf

have lost their lives. After the event the Indian Defense Forces are the recipients of harsh public criticism because they failed to discover the Pakistani forces until long after the border had been crossed.

A direct result of this is that Indian Government commits to constructing its own intelligence-gathering satellite TES (Technology Experiment Satellite), capable of producing images of objects as small as one meter. Israeli companies are substantial contributors and the satellite is completed in less than two year.[81]

India launches its first intelligence-gathering satellite from the island of Sriharikota off the west coast in October 2001. According to the Indian news agency Daily News & Analysis, TES is the first satellite that supplies images of central Afghanistan with resolution down to one meter to American forces when the invasion is launched in the same month.[82]

Since its establishment Svalsat has been highly engaged in attracting India as a customer. Svalsat bore the hope that the Indian Space Authorities would be the second contractual party after NASA, and that the agreements between NASA and the Indian Space Research Organisation ISRO would help in securing activities. It did not however work out quite like that. It isn't until Svalbard gets the fiber connection that the co-operation gains speed. By the summer of 2005 Svalbard Satellite Station has entered into agreements and received permits for seven Indian satellites, including TES.[83] This despite the fact that it should be a

---

[81]
http://web2.ges.gla.ac.uk/~gpetrie/Petrie_Space_Imaging_forGeospatial_Intellig ence_P38-45_GEO_03_07_LR.pdf

[82] http://www.dnaindia.com/india/report_india-s-spy-in-the-sky-by-2014_1345753

[83] Letter of Permit from Post- og teletilsynet, (The Norwegian Post and Telecommunications Authority) 17.06.05

well-known fact that TES can deliver images with one-meter resolution, and that these can, as is obvious to anyone, be used to identify enemy targets. Data from the Indian satellites is transmitted from Svalbard to India by fiber-optic cable.

Surprisingly, the following year the Norwegian authorities put a firm stop to this. Just before Christmas 2006 a new Indian satellite, Cartosat-2, is met with a point blank refusal. The satellite produces images with the same resolution as TES. The following is an excerpt from the letter of rejection:

> Cartosat-2 is equipped with a camera capable of producing optical images with a resolution of one meter. This provides a good basis for the identification of military targets. Images of this type can be used for targeting targets if the images are made available shortly after downloading, as could easily be the case when the images are transferred by fiber optic data transfer cable from Svalbard. The downloading and transfer of data in this way is deemed to be in conflict with the Treaty of Svalbard Article 9 and the Regulations governing the establishment, operation and use of ground stations for satellites of 11th June 1999.

The Governor of Svalbard has Inspectorate Authority for Svalsat the same year and discovers that the predecessor of Cartosat-2, Cartosat-1 – which also captures images with one meter resolution – has been downloading data to Svalbard without even having applied for a permit. This does not however result in fines or other legal remedies being imposed. Time passes, and both satellites are given permits on the proviso that data is delayed by 24 hours before being transmitted to India. India's first announced military intelligence gathering satellite, TES, can nonetheless use Svalsat's services without restriction.

The commercial sector of the Indian Space Authority, Antrix Corporation sells data rights for Cartosat-1 and a number of other Indian satellites to a multinational company, Space Imaging Group, as do both South Korea and Taiwan.[84] Space Imaging

Group uses data from several satellites with one meter resolution to make three-dimensional video animations of flyovers by aircraft of just about every location around the globe in order to "be able to prepare and implement air attacks".[85]

The American Navy is one of Space Imaging Group's customers. Can one be secure in the knowledge that a 24-hour delay in the data streams from Cartosat-1 and Cartosat-2 from Svalbard means that the data is no longer suited to such purpose? It's by no means unusual that there can be a lapse of several days from when a customer orders images of a defined area and until the satellite has been programmed, the images captured, downloaded and dispatched to the customer.

In the Norwegian Post and Telecommunications Authority's Annual Report for 2007 great concern was again expressed with regard to the regulation of satellite activities on Svalbard. Technology is developing so fast that the Norwegian Post and Telecommunications Authority believes that it's by no means impossible that one will be discussing issuing permits for a whole new generation of – according to the Authority the third generation – of satellites during the course of five years.

Examples of these are the satellites Radarsat-2 and TerraSar-X. The Authority writes:
"These (satellites) have the capacity to function in offensive military actions if the data retrieved from the satellites is available to users within a short space of time after downloading. Such use would be in conflict with the said regulations".

The Norwegian Post and Telecommunications Authority again takes up the dialogue with the Ministry of Foreign Affairs and agreement is reached to the effect that "prior to any decision concerning permits being taken, the Norwegian Space Centre (author's note: on behalf of Svalsat, author's note:) shows amongst

---

[84] See note 86

[85] http://www.satimagingcorp.com/svc/defense_mapping.html

other things how the delay in data transmission can be implemented". Radarsat-2 and TerraSar-X are nonetheless not subjected to the requirement to delay the transmission of data. So why all the concern about the Canadian Radarsat-2 and the German TerraSar-X?

During the war in Kosovo, Germany was dissatisfied with the lack of will on the part of the Americans to share intelligence they were gleaning from their own surveillance satellites. The USA has a restrictive policy on the sharing of this type of intelligence with allied countries, fearing that it may fall into the wrong hands. Germany strongly believed that the American policy was placing German lives in harm's way, and after the war reached the decision to create its own intelligence satellite system.[86]

One of the new German satellites is called TerraSar-X, and performs both commercial and military tasks. The Germans develop a technology package for TerraSar-X that until then had only been installed in top-secret military satellites.

The satellite can provide overview images of large areas and images with resolution down to one meter of selected areas under all light and weather conditions using radar (SAR), which can be aligned in any desired direction.

The satellite can track moving objects at ground level with its Ground Moving Target Indicator (GMTI). Image resolution is at the leading edge of development of commercial satellites. The combination of the extremely high image resolution, efficient coarse scanning of large areas and the satellites' ability to produce images regardless of weather and light conditions defines it as an excellent tool for military intelligence gathering. The technology for tracking objects at ground level – GMTI – can be directly implemented in hot military operations worldwide, and is currently under development for military activities in space. The hotly debated and controversial American intercontinental anti-nuclear missile attack defense system has shown interest in implementing

[86] http://www.acronym.org.uk/space/PE381369EN.pdf

the technology to track intercontinental missiles from space. The technology is being used by piloted American intelligence gathering aircraft such as Global Hawk and Joint Stars and unmanned American surveillance aircraft such as E-3 and E-8C.

For many years NATO has had a programme for exploiting SAR images in conjunction with GMTI, used for example to spot launches of short and medium distance missiles. The system has been tested in several NATO exercises, and Norway has been a participant in this development work. The Norwegian Defense Research Establishment has been carrying out research for many years on the exploitation of SAR technology. In the commercial sector GMTI may be used to monitor sea and road traffic. Speed monitoring is another potential option.

TerraSar-X is a joint project between the German state and the European industrial group Astrium. Astrium will hold the rights to international sales of data from TerraSar-X. A special law was passed for TerraSar-X, which is designed to ensure that the sale of data internationally will not impact on German security interests, and that information cannot fall into the hands of third parties and other routes. It may also transpire that the German authorities refuse to permit sales of data. The new act also makes it easier to import spares for TerraSar-X from the USA, parts that the USA have export restrictions for due to other security concerns. The German authorities are very well aware that if it falls into the wrong hands information and date generated by TerraSar-X could create major political and military headaches.[87]

In its marketing of TerraSar-X Astrium's subsidiary, Infoterra, makes no effort to conceal the fact that it is concentrating on reaching a global market for military intelligence – including during times of war. The following is a small extract from the company's Internet pages:

TerraSAR-X's unique capabilities make it an ideal sensor to support sensitive decision-making particularly in time-

[87] http://www.imagingnotes.com/go/article_free.php?mp_id=144

critical situations and can significantly augment the capabilities of armed forces and intelligence agencies, creating both tactical and strategic advantages.[88]

The USA is extremely interested in TerraSar-X. The military intelligence service National Geospatial-Intelligence Agency has commenced work on assessing how the data can be used by the American armed forces. There is interest in amongst other things how the data can be linked to intelligence and improved targeting of military targets.

American and German authorities enter into an agreement under which trials will be held to see if TerraSar-X can be used in connection with the planned and disputed American intercontinental anti-nuclear missile defense system. The USA will launch the satellite NFIRE, the task of which is to detect and monitor enemy missile launches. Part of the agreement is that Germany will supply laser technology to the satellite, which will be used to transmit the information. Germany and the USA are co-operating to find out if the information gathered by NFIRE can be relayed by laser to TerraSar-X and then to an earth station.[89]

The American Air Force is also interested. These results in that the American Congress, in the budgets for 2007 and 2008, allocate just over USD 1.5 million to enable US forces in combat to download TerraSar-X-data directly from the satellite.[90]

On 29th December 2009 the American intelligence service NGA issues a press release stating that from today's date it has signed a 5-year contract to purchase data from TerraSar-X with a

---

[88] http://infoterra.de/geo-intelligence
[89]

http://scitation.aip.org/getabs/servlet/GetabsServlet?prog=normal&id=IEECPS0 020090CP552000611000001&idtype=cvips&gifs=yes&ref=no

[90] http://www.dtic.mil/descriptivesum/Y2010/OSD/0605130D8Z.pdf

minimum worth of USD 10 000 and a maximum worth of USD 85 million. The contract also encompasses the sister-satellite Tandem-X. The NGA immediately places orders for satellite images. It is highly likely that TerraSar-X will earn a far greater sum than the minimum sum of USD 10 000 dollar from the contract. The contract was signed after the NGA has evaluated the results from TerraSar-X and discovered that the data is better or as good as the owners had stated.

In the brief press release from the NGA it says that the contract "will satisfy the NGA's, other intelligence services and the Pentagon's image requirements, as well as providing support to humanitarian actions and in other crises."[91]

The company that represents TerraSar-X in the USA, EADS North America, also issues a press release signed by CEO Sean O'Keefe. This is not quite so brief:

> This contract underscores EADS North America's ability to support the American soldier in combat and to assist our homeland security in that the company's enormous resources and advanced technology meets the standards and needs of our most demanding customers.

The press release also says that images and other products may be processed by departments in the Pentagon and other military intelligence services or be transmitted directly to war zones. Satellite images will be used by both national decision-makers as well as military units in combat situations.

At the same time a satellite similar to TerraSar-X is also awarded a contract with the intelligence service. The satellite is the Canadian Radarsat-2, the sequel to Radarsat-1. This is the other satellite the Norwegian Post and Telecommunications Authority is particularly skeptical to with regard to issuing a permit to use Svalbard.

---

[91] /www1.nga.mil/Newsroom/PressReleases/Press%20Releases/nga0912.pdf

The main fuselage of Radarsat-2 is five meters long and resembles a milk carton. The long, rectangular shape is necessary for the transmission of strong radar signals. Two rectangular panels are installed on both sides of the main fuselage. These are carriers for solar panels, the satellite's power supply. The total weight is 2.2 tons, and the satellite's orbit is 79 100 meters above sea level.

Radarsat-2 can also produce images under all weather conditions on a 24-hour basis and can track moving targets at ground level. Radarsat-2 has no need for concern that American intelligence only committed to purchasing USD 10 000 worth of images over a period of five years; The NGA starts ordering images immediately.

A report issued by a Canadian military research establishment in 2006 says that the technology for tracking targets at ground level, GMTI, was developed in joint project between the Canadian Defense Forces, Canadian space authorities and the privately-owned company MacDonald, Dettwiler and Associates, MDA, the owner of the satellite. The company has great expectations with regard to military use in the future.

The ability to track targets at ground level is by no means the only reason why USA and other intelligence services are so keen to obtain data from Radarsat-2. When it was launched in 2007 it only had the ability to produce images with three meters resolution. Since then adjustments to the data-streaming function has made it possible to produce images with one meter resolution. Work is ongoing to improve resolution even more.

The developers of Radarsat-2 were able to utilize experiences gleaned with its predecessor Radarsat-1, the first satellite that used radar to produce images and sell data in the international marketplace. In the case of Radarsat-1 there was often a delay of several days from the placing of an order for images and until these were delivered. The delay for Radarsat-2 has been considerably reduced. This is often a key factor for military intelligence.

Further, Radarsat-2 has a number of technical innovations, for example the ability to sweep the radar beam from side to side, allowing the satellite to scan and image larger areas.

Data from Radarsat-2 is intended for use in the international marketplace, and prior to the launch the USA had very serious concerns that non-friendly states such as Iraq would come into possession of images from the satellite. It would have caused irreparable damage if Iraq had got its hands on Radarsat images of American forces in the Middle East. NASA, the launch enterprise, delayed the launch operation and negotiations between the USA and Canada were entered into. In June of 2000 the American Secretary of State Madeleine Albright and the Canadian Foreign Minister Lloyd Axworthy signed an agreement on Radarsat. The most important point is paragraph 1, which secures military control of the Canadian radar system for the USA:

> The parties agree to ensure that such commercial long-range measuring systems shall be controlled by each of the parties in a comparable manner with the purpose of protecting and serving joint and common national and foreign policy interests.

The agreement illustrates Radarsat's military security importance, and that the USA has secured control of the satellite system. Radarsat-2 is launched in December 2007 from Vandenberg Air Force Base in California. Case Managers with the Norwegian Post and Telecommunications Authority are still considering whether or not to grant a permit for Radarsat-2 to use Svalbard.

Half a year later – and long before the agreement with the American intelligence service NGA was signed –Radarsat-2 has already sold "about 5000 images and other data products to American authorities". This is quoted from an article written by Director Wide Larsson in the company that owns Radarsat 2, MacDonald, Dettwiler and Associates in the journal Imaging Notes in the autumn of 2008. He also writes that the Americans will be using the data "to support a large number of tasks and missions at sea and on land throughout a broad range of intelligence and defense apparatus. This includes guided ammunition, identifying targets, assessing threats, data on changes over a large land and sea areas and maritime surveillance". He makes no attempt to hide the fact that military intelligence is one of the satellites' main tasks:

> It has been especially designed for operational use for intelligence that has established very ambitious goals. The satellite's enormous data-gathering capacity, flexibility in imagery, detailed information data [...] puts it at the forefront of commercial satellites for modern defense and intelligence aims.[92]

Data from Radarsat-2 is used by the Americans in the actions in Afghanistan and in Iraq. In the case of the Army's 1st Space Battalion, Commercial Exploitation Team (CET), Radarsat-2 has been the only satellite with the capability to provide images under "just about any weather conditions imaginable, day or night and even during sandstorms". According to the 1st Space Battalion the Battalion plays a key role in the planning and leadership of military operations in ground combat.[93]

It is not however solely the USA that has signed agreements with Radarsat-2. China is also a customer, despite the limitations on the sale of images incorporated in the agreement between the USA and Canada on Radarsat-2. There is little doubt that China's access to images from Radarsat-2 is of import to that country's military strength. The Pentagon's 2007 report to Congress on China's military capabilities and capacity says that: "Radarsat and other commercial satellites are a necessary part of that country's intelligence." Radarsat is for example vital if Chinese forces aim to identify and strike at American marine forces in the Western Pacific.

---

[92] http://www.imagingnotes.com/go/article_free.php?mp_id=147
[93] http://www.dtic.mil/cgi-bin/GetTRDoc?Location=U2&doc=GetTRDoc.pdf&AD=ADA521118

Norway is the first European country to enter into an agreement with Radarsat-2. The agreement is signed as early as in 2003, long before the satellite was sent into earth orbit. Norway commits to purchasing satellite images for USD ten millions, and to exchange technology and other forms of industrial co-operation with the Canadian industrial partner, MDA, and the Norwegian party, Kongsberg Spacetec.

The Norwegian Defense Forces are the largest user of Radarsat-1, and immediately commence using Radarsat-2 when the satellite becomes operational and data can be downloaded in Tromsø. The Defense Forces have a powerful toll in a satellite that supplies images with one meter resolution and has other resources for identification, particularly in the identification of all types of vessels in Norwegian sovereign waters – which, against the background of the clarification of the eastern boundaries with Russia – is several times larger than the Norwegian land masses.

The Norwegian Defense Research Establishment, (FFI), has a number of ongoing research projects and development projects concerned with the exploitation of data from Radarsat-2. The FFI has used data from Radarsat-2 during a number of NATO exercises. During the NATO exercise Cold Response in Inner Troms (Northern Norway) in 2009, the Norwegian Defense Research Establishment tested all potential uses in a completely new unit that is under development, the Norwegian Defense Satellite and GeoInformation Centre (FSGI). The FSGI was planned under the auspices of the military intelligence service and the Norwegian Defense Military Geographic Service, and will be operated by the last-mentioned.

In mid-March 2009 7500 soldiers from 14 nations were stationed in large sections of the County of Troms in Northern Norway ready to commence combat training. The Norwegian armed forces had access to supplies of images from Radarsat-2 under a previous agreement. The images were requisitioned from Kongsberg Satellite Services in Tromsø, who downloaded the images ordered and transmitted these on the buyer. The exercise also purchased a number of images from several commercial satellites, including Kompsat-2 and Radarsat-2.

Radarsat-2 flew over the area during the hours of darkness in the early morning and evening, but was nonetheless able to capture good images. The NATO exercise ordered and received five images of The Balsfjord during the final days of the exercise. It was vital that in combat situations the images were the most recent possible in order to be of practical use. The prime aim was to deliver the images to the military four hours after the images were captured in order for them to be recent enough to have practical military worth. All five images from Radarsat-2 were delivered in less than four hours from image capture.[94]

The Norwegian Post and Telecommunications Authority was consistent in its skepticism to issuing a permit to Radarsat-2 to use Svalsat. Well over a year passes from the time the application was submitted in January 2007 and until the permit was issued in October 2008. The Norwegian Defense Research Establishment is aware that with Radarsat-2's technical specification and Svalbard's new fiber cable, Svalsat can be a key participant in combat situations.[95]

The formal applicant for a permit for Radarsat-2 is the Norwegian Space Centre, even though the application concerns Svalbard Satellite Station's, permission to communicate with Radarsat-2. This gives me food for thought. The Norwegian Space Centre is a public administrative organ, and I fail to understand that a public administrative organ can apply on behalf of a private, commercial enterprise, Kongsberg Satellite Services (KSAT), the owner of Svalbard Satellite Station. KSAT has joint ownership; it's 50 percent owned by the Kongsberg Group and 50 percent by the Ministry of Trade and Industry. The Norwegian Space Centre

---

[94] http://rapporter.ffi.no/rapporter/2009/00815.pdf

[95] Evaluation in connection with Post- og teletilsynets (The Norwegian Post and Telecommunications Authority)
case processing of the permit for Radarsat-2

manages the Ministry of Trade and Industry's ownership interest. The Norwegian Space Centre's explanation of this is that it was previously a foundation, and that the arrangement continued after the Space Centre became a public administrative organ.[96] I don't feel much wiser after hearing this answer. I suspect that it can be very convenient for the Norwegian Space Centre to have a choice of hats. Here's why:

The Norwegian Space Centre became aware of Norwegian Post and Telecommunications Authority's strong skepticism with regard to issuing a permit for Radarsat-2 through e-mails dated 13th and 14th August 2007. In its letter of reply the Space Centre calls attention to and emphasizes that an agreement has been signed with Canadian authorities on Radarsat-2 including plans for the downloading of data on Svalbard. The Space Centre is using an agreement the Norwegian Space Centre has entered into with Canada on behalf of Norway to med Canada in the application process to ensure that the commercial enterprise KSAT is awarded a permit. The dividing line between the Norwegian Space Centre as a public administrative organ and the Norwegian Space Centre as a commercial enterprise has been erased.

The Space Centre and KSAT realize that compromises must be reached if a permit is to be issued. In the letter referred to above the Space Centre proposes that the Canadian satellite shall not be allowed to downstream images with technology to track moving objects or images with the highest resolution. Nothing is mentioned about the Norwegian Post and Telecommunications Authority's and the Ministry of Foreign Affair's mandatory requirement that the data must be delayed in order to avoid the data stream representing a breach of the Treaty of Svalbard.

The Norwegian Defense Research Establishment then supports the issuance of a permit for Radarsat-2. The question is whether these assessments are in this case impartial and independent. As we have seen previously, the Norwegian Defense

---

[96] Director of Communications Marianne Moen of Norsk Romsenter (The Norwegian Space Centre)

Research Establishment and the Defense Forces are already deeply involved in co-operation with Radarsat on the exploitation of images obtained by the satellites for both research and military purposes.

The Norwegian Post and Telecommunications Authority remains skeptical to issuing a permit for Radarsat-2. This skepticism is reinforced by that the Governor of Svalbard, who is responsible for ensuring that the requirements in permits are adhered to, has said that it is difficult to carry out his inspectorate tasks. As early as in 2005 the Governor took the initiative to an evaluation of the inspection arrangement, and followed this up the next year with new input relating to both the inspections and the general regulations.[97] It was in the same year that it was found that some satellites were operating without any form of permit. Nothing was however done about this.

The Norwegian Post and Telecommunications Authority makes the point: While there had previously been "a focus on whether a satellite could be accepted as compatible with the Treaty of Svalbard's Article 9, it is now a question of which parts of satellite activities can be accepted in the light of Article 9". The Norwegian Post and Telecommunications Authority is skeptical to how the Governor will be able to check that Radarsat-2 does not downstream illegal data to Svalsat.

It is perhaps not unexpected that Deputy Director General Knut E. Myrvang of the Norwegian Space Centre replies thus: "This is not a problem", He says that this is easily checked by reading the orders for data and taking random samples of the downloaded data. Is this opinion put forward on behalf of the administrative organ or the commercial enterprise?

The Norwegian Post and Telecommunications Authority then sends the whole case to the Ministry of Foreign Affairs. On 10th October 2008 the Norwegian Space Centre receives a yes to its application for Radarsat-2. Svalsat is granted permission to

---

[97] Annual Report, the Governor of Svalbard, 2006

transmit signals to the satellite for maintenance and guidance of the satellite as well as to download signals to store images. Svalsat is not however allowed to download data for tracking moving objects or data with maximum resolution.

No conditions were imposed for delaying the data stream, although the Norwegian Post and Telecommunications Authority and the Ministry of Foreign Affairs were previously of the opinion this was an absolute necessity if the downloads were not to be in breach of the Treaty of Svalbard. In addition to that Svalbard uses Radarsat-2 earth stations in amongst other places China and Canada, as well as direct downloading in war zones such as Afghanistan and Iraq.

The German satellite TerraSar-X – which has many technical similarities to Radarsat-2 – has also given the Norwegian Post and Telecommunications Authority a headache. As previously mentioned, the Authority is of the opinion that this satellite is also in conflict with the Treaty of Svalbard in that it can be used for warlike purposes.

The Norwegian Space Centre sent its application for TerraSar-X on 25th April 2007. The application does not mention the military applications:

> The application is sent by the German Space Centre DLR and the commercial enterprise Infoterra GmbH, which is a private - public co-operation between DLR and the company EADS Astrium. Under the terms of the co-operative agreement DLR is responsible for downloading data for scientific users, and Infoterra for commercial users. All data from the satellite is freely available on commercial terms.

Images that can be purchased by anyone have little or no military importance. But is data commercially available? Not according to an article written by three employees of the German Space Centre DLR, in the journal Imaging Notes:

Data gathered by TerraSar-X is of a quality that until very recently was only produced by secret military satellites. Such data is of import to security. The effects of weapons systems and political threats can be greatly amplified with the aid of such earth observation data. […] Security must be given due attention in the production and distribution. […] If checks of requests to purchase data show that there is cause for concern for security reasons, this will result in […] limitations on the use and sale of images for certain areas, the use of downloading stations, the use of defined image formats in limitations on the processing of the data stream.

The Norwegian Space Centre was made aware of the Norwegian Post and Telecommunications Authority's high degree of skepticism with regard to issuing a permit, and proposes that permission to command the satellite from Svalbard should be withheld, and that data downloaded to Svalsat shall be delayed by two hours before forwarding.

The Norwegian Post and Telecommunications Authority still fears that the data can be sold on and used in conflict with the Treaty of Svalbard and expresses deep concern with regard to how the Governor – who is responsible for ensuring that operations are in accordance with the permit – will be able to check that data is actually delayed. The Norwegian Space Centre is of the opinion that the delays can easily be monitored by checking the logs. This once again raises the question of whether the Norwegian Space Centre is commenting in its role as a public authority or a commercial enterprise. The case is now returned to the Ministry of Foreign Affairs for a final decision.

On 9th February 2009 TerraSar-X is granted a permit to download data to Svalsat. The sole precondition is that data is delayed at Svalsat for at least two hours before onward transmission; in the majority of cases a shorter period of time than the majority of potential users thought would not pose a problem. This notwithstanding, the German satellite owners react strongly to the limitation. They appeal the decision to the Norwegian authorities and take the matter up with the German Ministry of Foreign Affairs.

The Ministry of Transport and Communications receives the case for the processing of the appeal and seeks advice from a number of ministries and departments, including the Ministry of Foreign Affairs. Even though the Ministry of Transport and Communications is aware that the Norwegian Defense Research Establishment is of the opinion that a delay is necessary in order to maintain Norway's commitments, the Ministry repeals the precondition. The grounds given are commercial regards and that the ruling states there is "room for relaxing the authorities' self-imposed "assurances in connection with the administration of earth stations", which in plain English means a more liberal interpretation of the regulations.

Currently there are no restrictions governing TerraSar-X's use of Svalsat in relation to the downloading and storage of data for the production of images at maximum resolution or the production of data for tracking moving objects at ground level. This means that – as an example – five minutes after TerraSar-X has passed over Afghanistan, data on troop movements has been downloaded by Svalsat and is ready for use in guiding weaponry in the combat zones. Even the Norwegian Defense Research Establishment disagrees with Norway's enforcement of the Treaty of Svalbard with regard to this application.[98]

---

[98] The Ministry of Transport and Communications appeal concerning TerraSar-X, 02.11.10

Chapter 7
Controlling signals from Svalbard for pilotless combat aircraft in Afghanistan?

A group of American specialists arrives in Longyearbyen mid-June 2007. In the course of the next three weeks they will erect two antennas for completely new tasks at Svalsat on Platåberget. The group of six work for the military section of the American Boeing Group.

Acclimatizing to Svalbard is not an easy matter for the six American specialists. All are from the southern states, and the leader of the group, Tom Valentine – a big, burly character around 40 with a dark, bushy beard – is from Chandler, Arizona, on the Mexican border, with summer temperatures well over 40 degrees Celsius. In Longyearbyen it's not unusual for temperatures in June and July to tip below zero.

After the long trip another shock is in store: It's almost impossible to find a place to stay. Before departure there had been a good deal of uncertainty about the date of departure, and the Americans had not booked accommodation. They should have done. At this time of year Svalbard is in the midst of a hectic tourist season and all accommodation is fully booked. They can forget about staying at the same place the next three weeks. It is only by the skin of their teeth that they manage to find a roof over their heads, and suitcases are shuttled frequently between the various accommodations. The standard varies radically.

And then there's the Midnight Sun. Tom Valentine and the others are grateful for the obligatory blackout curtains that keep the light out. Nonetheless it's almost impossible to sleep. A long, arduous journey, time difference, extreme change in temperature and problems with sleep means a week has passed before the Americans recover. However this doesn't really interfere with the job they have come to do: Subcontractors spend the first week finishing the foundations on which the antennas will be erected. There's not that much for the Americans to do until the foundations are in place.

The antennas were previously sited on Egilsstadhir, Iceland. Another team from Boeing disassembled the equipment and sent it by boat to Longyearbyen, which has a much better position than Iceland to communicate with satellites over the North Pole. The Americans think the assignment on Svalbard is exotic, but also hazardous – that includes the drive from accommodation in Longyearbyen to Svalsat. The group has great respect for the narrow road up the mountainside to Platåberget, which even at this time of year can be slippery and icy. Tom Valentine is the permanent driver of the work vehicle as he has previously been in Alaska. Their fears are not lessened when they see wheel tracks that show how close to the edge they have been when driving back and forth.

A crane hoists the two three-meter long antennas into the correct position on the top of two four-meter high steel constructions. The whole process must be carried out with exact precision. Both the foundation and antenna system are covered with canvas to protect against weather and wind. The plant is due to be tested already 5th July, and the Americans work under pressure together with local subcontractors. The last few days they work around the clock, and up on the plateau the weather can change in a matter of minutes from blue skies to fog with almost zero visibility. The type of weather polar bears find ideal to hunt in, but which understandably the Americans are not so impressed with. They are fully aware there are around 3,000 polar bears on the archipelago, and do not totally rely on assurances that at this time of year the polar bears have migrated further east to hunt seals.

Despite some technical problems the antenna system is sited, and testing of the plant is successful. "You can imagine how happy we were. Everyone had made an extra effort and solved all the challenges. It was in fact a good experience. Our focus was

91

firmly on doing a proper job within the time limit," said Tom Valentine.[99]

The group works for Boeing Integrated Defense System, which is a part of the Boeing group. Boeing is most well-known for its commercial passenger aircraft, but is also the world's third largest arms manufacturer with a turnover of USD 30 billion per annum.[100] Boeing is the principal supplier for the controversial U.S. intercontinental nuclear missile defense and also supplies engineering services and maintenance for the intercontinental nuclear missile system Minuteman III, which is the United States' most significant land-based nuclear weapon. Boeing's close ties with the U.S. Defense is the reason why the Norwegian Government Pension Fund Global, also known as the 'Oil Fund' does not invest in the group on ethical grounds.

The antennas Boeing Integrated Defense Systems set up on Svalbard in 2007 and 2008 couple Svalbard up with a network of communication satellites for speech, text and data transfer that is unparalleled – Iridium. The Iridium system consists of 66 active satellites that function in the same way as mobile antennas on the ground. The ground equipment for Iridium is coupled up against Iridium satellites in the same way as when you drive your car and talk on your mobile by linking automatically between the stations. Iridium satellites cover the whole world and can also exchange signals amongst themselves.

At the opening of a similar Iridium ground station in Fairbanks, Alaska, in August 2006, Joe Ralston, former deputy leader for the Joint Chiefs of Staff – the advisory organ for den American President – held a short speech where he stressed the importance of the station for the U.S. Defense: "Our soldiers on the ground, in the air and at sea across the globe rely on Iridium

---

[99] http://www.boeing.com/news/frontiers/archive/2008/feb/ts_sf02.pdf

[100] The Sipri Top 100 arms-producing companies, 2008

every day for reliable and secure communication throughout the command chain."

Nothing was said about Iridium's military significance when Iridium started operating on Norwegian territory.[101]

The U.S. Defense is Iridium's biggest customer, and the relationship between Iridium and the Pentagon has been close throughout the company's brief history.[102] Autumn 1999 Iridium was on the brink of bankruptcy after just nine months' operation due to major investment costs. This displeased the Pentagon greatly. The military communication satellites only covered half the military's requirements for satellite communication. Iridium provided telephone connections all over the planet, which was especially important for the U.S. Navy and specialist forces. The Pentagon then entered into a two-year agreement on the purchase of services for NOK 500 million, plus an agreement that the Pentagon would participate in developing telephone connections that were impossible to tap into. The agreement also stated that co-operation on the purchase of services could be extended to seven years with a framework figure of more than NOK 3 billion. The agreements between Iridium and the Pentagon in 2000 secured continued operation of the satellite system.[103]

In the following years Iridium co-operates closely with different sections of the U.S. Defense to make the satellite system more serviceable for military purposes. In 2002 a division in the U.S. Navy, the Marine Corps Weapons Laboratory, had responsibility for developing portable communication systems for the U.S. Navy. This entailed an upgrading of the U.S. Defense's satellite station on Hawaii and for the first time handheld, tactical UHF receivers/senders for the Navy, which were used in Iraq and Afghanistan.[104]

101

http://www.spacedaily.com/reports/Senator_Ted_Stevens_Officiates_At_New_I
ridium_Satellite_Ground_Station_In_Alaska_999.html

102 http://siliconinvestor.advfn.com/readmsg.aspx?msgid=25999900
103 http://abcnews.go.com/Technology/story?id=119255&page=1

In 2003 the Pentagon entered into a new agreement with Iridium that secured the Pentagon's use of the satellite network for another two years. The military leaders were now keen that Iridium satellites no longer should be used to send sound and data from one station to another, but also from one to many. In 2006 Iridium had in cooperation with another division of the U.S. Defense, Warfighting Laboratory, installed new data programs in their satellites and renewed ground equipment. This led to new, major co-operation contracts between Iridium and the Pentagon.

A new, decisive instrument for American soldiers in Afghanistan and Iraq is the "Distributed Tactical Communications System" (DTCS), which is based on new data programs for Iridium satellites and improved communication between the different parts of the satellite system.

With DTCS the soldiers can by merely pressing a letter on a keyboard speak to, or send data via satellite to, thousands of others in an operation, or to a command center and receive replies without any risk of eavesdropping.

The system is not dependent on direct visibility to receivers, as is the case with many other communication systems. This has proven to be very useful in the mountain areas of Afghanistan. The data information can for example be one's own position, which thus also can immediately be conveyed to other soldiers close by or to key command centers.

There have been concrete situations in valleys in Afghanistan where American soldiers have not had direct visibility to satellites over the Equator, and DTCS was the only option available to call for help. In 2010 the Americans had 3500 DTCS ground units in Iraq and Afghanistan.[105]

---

[104] http://www.defensestandard.com/DS%20Edit%20V8/SATCOM.pdf
[105] http://iridiumeverywhere.com/IE_PS.html

Iridium and other private companies are becoming increasingly important in meeting the U.S. Defense's growing need for satellite communication. In 2002 the U.S. Defense and other public institutions purchased satellite communication for around NOK 2 billion. This figure increased to NOK 4 billion in 2008. 20 years ago the Pentagon almost always only used their own satellites for communication. Private companies now supply between 80 and 90 percent of all satellite communication.

Among the principal reasons for the steadily increasing demand is the desire to spread information to a greater extent to all combat participants, increased use of satellite-based sensors and pilotless aircraft and other pilotless arms systems that are dependent on receiving and sending massive volumes of data without time lag.

From 2006 to 2009 – under President George W. Bush – there were 41 American attacks carried out by pilotless aircraft or so-called drones in Pakistan, which killed 454 terrorists and civilians. In 2009 – under President Obama – there were about as many as in the three preceding years, 42 attacks, and the number killed at least 453. Add to this the attacks in Afghanistan and Iraq. For example Predator and Reaper aircraft executed 244 weapons launches in the two countries during 2007 and 2008.[106]

Iridium has been used by U.S. pilotless intelligence aircraft in Iraq and Afghanistan, including the Tiger Shark, Silver Fox and Mako aircraft.[107] In fact, pilotless helicopters have now been developed for military intelligence and surveillance, controlled via Iridium. The pilotless intelligence aircraft can be employed in operations that are considered hazardous for piloted aircraft. In relation to piloted intelligence aircraft the pilotless intelligence aircraft are also relatively moderate in price.

---

[106] http://www.bbc.co.uk/news/world-south-asia-10648909

[107] http://www.dodsbir.net/SuccessStories/display_story.asp?id=SS00000419

The Norwegian Armed Forces has recently acquired 45 pilotless intelligence gathering aircraft, roughly the same size as model aircraft, for use by ground forces in Afghanistan. The aircraft will be guided in part by signals transmitted directly between operator and aircraft. The manufacturer makes little comment in relation to information about the use of satellite communication.

What then is the story with pilotless combat aircrafts' use of Iridium in Afghanistan and Pakistan? One thing is clear; NATO has considered using Tiger Shark aircraft and the Iridium satellite constellation to release bombs by parachute. Tiger Shark has a wingspan of around five meters, is about five meters long and can remain airborne twelve hours without refueling. The aircraft was developed for the U.S. Special Command.[108]

Enormous data capacity is required to control and carry out attacks with pilotless combat aircraft. For this reason the military forces in Afghanistan prefer to use civilian communication satellites that utilize the Ka-band instead of the L-band, which Iridium satellites currently use.[109] But in the course of the next two-three years Iridium will also be able to offer services on the Ka-band.[110] Iridium is now developing a whole new generation of satellites, Iridium NEXT, and space has already been reserved on Platåberget, Longyearbyen, for new antennas to serve the new satellites.[111]

---

[108] http://www.nps.edu/Academics/Centers/ADSC/papers/JPADS%20-%20Benney%20-%20DOD%20New%20JPADS%20Programs%20and%20NATO%20Activities.pdf

[109] UAV Satellite Datalink Global Supply & Demand – A state of the Art, London Satellite Exchange

[110] http://www.defenseindustrydaily.com/Iridium-NEXT-Boosting-Data-Speeds-Improving-DoD-Space-Awareness-06161/

[111] Sten-Christian Pedersen, Managing Director of Svalsat, to *Svalbardposten*, *(The Svalbard Post)* 1st October 2010

Thales Alenia Space, which is a European company with branches in France, Spain, Italy and Belgium, has been awarded a contract to build 81 satellites for a total price of NOK 13 billion.[112] The Pentagon is eager to use spare capacity from Iridium NEXT on 40 to 60 development projects planned for outer space.[113]

Iridium makes no secret of the fact that Svalbard is important to the company's further expansion, and a central component of Iridium's global network. "The new station in Norway is the latest contribution to achieving top performance in our network of satellites. This will enable us to continue as the only company that can offer secure, global communication," says Managing Director Matt Desch.[114]

Iridium has a short history on Svalbard. It was not until February 2007 that the news broke that Iridium intended to establish itself at Svalsat. Iridium and KSAT then issued a press release saying that the companies had agreed on the construction of two antennas for guiding and commanding Iridium satellites and downloading data from satellites. At this point the work with the new antennas was well underway,[115] even though NPT permission arrives several months later.[116] The permit gives Iridium free rein, even though Iridium with its format of a network of communication satellites represents something entirely new on Svalbard.

---

[112]
http://www.aviationweek.com/aw/generic/story_generic.jsp?channel=space&id=news/asd/2010/10/29/10.xml&headline=Iridium%20Satellite%20Contract%20Takes%20Effect

[113] http://spaceflightnow.com/news/n1003/27iridium/

[114] http://www.prnewswire.com/news-releases/iridiumr-satellite-to-open-new-ground-station-in-norway-58127232.html

[115] *Svalbardposten, (The Svalbard Post)* 16th February 2007
[116] Post- og teletilsynets (The Norwegian Post and Telecommunications Authority) permit for Iridium, 27.04.07

Once again it is proximity to the North Pole and the fiber connection that is crucial. Iridium already has ground stations elsewhere for instance in Fairbanks, Alaska and Iqaluit, Canada, but none of the stations lie far enough north to track all the passes over the North Pole. The U.S. Defense has its own Iridium station at Wahiawa in Hawaii.[117] The fiber connection enables the Hawaiian station to communicate directly with Iridium satellites via Svalsat.[118] The military Iridium station in Hawaii is in direct contact with combat operations globally. The Pentagon has further plans for the station. As late as November 2010 Iridium signed a contract with the Pentagon on the modernization of the plant budgeted to cost NOK 75 million. In a press release issued in connection with the contract, Iridium stressed the significance satellites and the entire ground system have for warfare: Iridium's global satellite network and supporting infrastructure on the ground provide vital lines of communication for U.S. forces and civilian authorities around the globe, according to Scott Scheimreif, Vice President of Iridium.[119]

Iridium satellites are also utilized in the further development of the GPS system, which has become indispensable for almost all U.S. warfare – from guiding arms to navigation. Boeing and Iridium, with support from the Pentagon, are collaborating to exploit the 66 Iridium satellites to achieve greater precision in GPS applications, and at the same time make it more difficult for an enemy to block or jam GPS signals.[120]

Iridium is heavily involved in key elements of the U.S. war machine. In the space of four years five antennas have been erected on Svalbard to serve the satellites,[121] and there are plans for even

---

[117]

http://www.spacedaily.com/reports/Pentagon_Contracts_Iridium_to_Upgrade_Satellite_Communications_Gateway_999.html

[118] See note 113
[119] [119] http://files.shareholder.com/downloads/ABEA-3ERWFI/1389868740x0x417921/6701ce93-92d5-4990-82d0-5b380d74070f/IRDM_News_2010_11_11_Company_News.pdf
[120] http://www.iridiumeverywhere.com/archives/Vol_4_Issue_2/IE_DTB.html

more antennas to serve a new generation of satellites. More exotic trips could well be on the agenda for Boeing staff in the years ahead.

---

[121] *Svalbardposten, (The Svalbard Post)* 1st October 2010

Chapter 8
Svalsat supports Norwegian forces in Afghanistan

On one of my many trips taken in connection with work on this book I had to wait six hours at Tromsø Airport for my next flight. Many a time I've seen business people and others set themselves up with a laptop to make the best of some spare time, but I had never actually done that myself. At least not until now. Something the Assistant Governor of Svalbard, Lars Fause, had said to me had played on my mind:

If satellites that are linked to Svalbard are used by Norwegian forces in Afghanistan, it is a clear breach of the Svalbard Treaty. In this connection Norway is at war, and Svalbard is in that case used for warlike purposes. No doubt about that.

Is there a connection between satellite activity on Svalbard and Norwegian warfare in Afghanistan? I have to get to the bottom of this. If Svalbard is used in Norwegian war efforts in Afghanistan, it is yet another heavy argument for a breach of the Svalbard Treaty. The authorities cannot then continue to hide behind inadequate insight to data such as downloads or how these are employed. I have to find myself a quiet corner in the airport.

The wall at the end of the entrance hall at Tromsø Airport faces Kvaløy Bridge and the island of Kvaløya with its magnificent mountain formations. Avinor have very wisely placed a few comfortable chairs close to power points by the panorama windows. Today a low-lying autumn sun has tinted the snow-clad mountains a delicate shade of pink. A brilliant blue sky above completes the scene. Just the place for me to sit and work. I log on using the airport's wireless network.

I concentrate on two satellite systems, the German Rapid Eye and the Italian COSMO-SkyMed, both of which utilize Svalsat.[122] These two satellite systems are the first in the world comprised of a fleet of satellites that fly in formation and capture images of the whole planet. Formation flying facilitates the high frequent capture of images of selected regions, a characteristic that can prove advantageous for intelligence services during war operations.

First I want to take a look at Rapid Eye. It is the converted intercontinental Russian nuclear missile DNEPR-1 that launches and positions the five Rapid Eye-satellites in orbit from the missile launch installation Plesetsk, Archangel, on Friday 29 August 2008. A press release from Kongsberg Satellite Services a few days later draws my attention. Excerpt from press release: "All data from the satellite system for the entire satellite system's lifetime shall be downloaded on Svalbard. These satellites [...] shall provide image data of flowering, growth and maturing of vegetation and cultivated fields from all over the world, and will also be of use in foreign aid and natural disasters." The previous year KSAT had received permission from the NPT to communicate with Rapid Eye – without restrictions. To all appearances it is a purely civilian project.

It is certainly correct that Rapid Eye is utilized for important civilian purposes, but the advanced satellite system is also used by military units in many countries. Right from the start it was clear the German armed forces would be using Rapid Eye. Since then the system has been marketed globally. The following is an excerpt from a presentation written by Wade Larson, marketing director of MDA Space Operations, which has the sales rights to Rapid Eye: "This new generation of commercial satellites can provide the defense and intelligence communities with

---

[122] see http://www.sjokart.no/Norge_digitalt/Norsk/Motesteder/Arbeidsgrupper/AG_Sa tellittdata/Referater/filestore/Norge_Digitalt_ny/Mtesteder/Arbeidsgrupper/Fagg ruppe_satellittdata/Stver-Isaksen-KSAT_Faggruppesatellittdata.pdf and Bo Andersen: "Rommet som plattform. Med øye for Jorda og den tredje dimensjon", (With space as the platform – and an eye on Earth and the Third Dimension) Norsk Romsenter (The Norwegian Space Centre), 12.02.09

powerful broad area monitoring and surveillance capabilities, high revisit cycles, and lower costs.[123]

Special emphasis is given in the marketing to the fact the satellites capture images of the same region at 20-minute intervals: "This high revisit time is relevant for warfighter support."

Customers were quick to contact the company after the press release. Rapid Eye is among other things used to monitor the building of nuclear installations in Iran the last few years. The following is an excerpt from an interview with the Vice President of MDA, David Hargreaves, uploaded on Rapid Eye's website:

> We already do change detection for a lot of our customers. But the idea for a lot of military users is to use Rapid Eye as a wide-area surveillance capability, which really triggers things that are interesting to them that then can be looked at with higher resolution assets.[124]

In 2009 Rapid Eye entered into a co-operation with the American company MakaLani on sale of data directed at "the U.S. authorities, in particular defense, intelligence and national security authorities".[125] The military intelligence unit National Geospatial-Intelligence Agency is also interested in purchasing images from Rapid Eye.

I have had confirmed that Rapid Eye is undeniably suited to military purposes, marketed for active use in warfare and has a number of military customers. But I haven't been able to prove that Rapid Eye has contracts with American intelligence or other

---

[123] http://www.imagingnotes.com/ee_downloads/Imaging%20Notes%202008%20Fall.pdf

[124] http://www.rapideye.de/upload/documents/articles/GIF_-_Worldwide_Imagery.pdf

[125] http://satellite.tmcnet.com/topics/satellite/articles/63021-makalani-partners-with-21st-century-systems-market-geospatial.htm

defense departments, and neither have I found links to American or Norwegian warfare in Afghanistan, even though this could have naturally been the case regardless.

I look at my watch, and realize I have to give up this lead if I am to manage to find a connection between Svalbard and Norwegian warfare in Afghanistan before I have to catch my flight.

I concentrate instead on the Italian satellite system COSMO-SkyMed, which received a permit to utilize Svalbard for earth observation in 2005, and was renewed in 2009. The satellite system is one of the most advanced that has received a permit to use Svalbard.

As with Radarsat-2 and TerraSar-X this satellite system can also capture images with a resolution just less than a meter under all lighting conditions because the satellite captures images with radar and not with the aid of sunlight. The COSMO-SkyMed constellation consists of four satellites that fly in formation around the earth. In this way the satellites can capture images of every single square meter of the globe earth with one meter's resolution at least twice every twenty-four hours, regardless of lighting conditions. Five times per twenty-four hours over the Barents Sea. No other commercial satellites can do that. The satellite system is ideally suited to detecting all kinds of movement on the ground, including for example troop movements.

I Google the combination "COSMO-SkyMed", "intelligence", "early warning". I quickly find web pages that show the sales company for satellites, the half-State owned Italian company e-GEOS, makes no attempt to hide that this satellite system is also looking to attract military customers. I enter the company's website:

Intelligence
Surveillance for intelligence purposes and early warning are among the most important means to achieve an effective defense. It requires analyses of possible threats

103

and continual monitoring of objects and events that can trigger crises. In order to monitor critical plant/installations, factories for mass destruction arms and illegal activities connected to conflict resources such as mining activity and forestry requires images with high resolution.

The SAR technology and COSMO-SkyMed in particular are ideally suited to these purposes, given that crises are often located around the tropical latitudes where it is difficult to use other types of satellites due to frequent occurrences of cloud bases.

Searching by use of a key word is one way of finding information on Google. Another way is to combine key words in text with a web address or parts of a web address. There's no getting around the fact that the United States is very often deeply involved in the latest advances in space, and I'm eager to find out what official American sites have to say about COSMO-SkyMed. Very many websites and documents with connections to the U.S. Defense have the letters "mil" as the net address. In that way I receive official military information that I can – from experience – rely on as correct.

Often in this context it can be a good idea to write in the word "unclassified" to obtain information that may be of a sensitive nature, as strange as that may sound. The reason is that many of these documents have been assessed in relation to being kept secret and therefore they can be of interest.

I search for COSMO-SkyMed, combined with the words "intelligence", "mil" and "unclassified". I glance over the first ten documents that turn up, without any catching my interest. Among the next ten a web address turns up with a beginning that is very familiar: www.dtic.mil/descriptivesum.

The net address contains the official budgets for the Pentagon and often provides detailed descriptions of what the money is allocated to. The document I retrieve states the Pentagon spent around one million dollars in 2009 and 2010 to enable it to

104

utilize COSMO-SkyMed in the American armed forces. It also states "For the warfighter and mission planner, this capability will provide four times the surveillance capability at an eighth of the resolution, along with quad polarization." [126]

Lying by my side is the permit given by the NPT to COSMO-SkyMed, which also provides some information about the satellite's tasks:

> Environmental surveillance
> Town and regional planning
> Management and monitoring of natural resources
> Observations of agricultural areas and forests
> Monitoring of natural disasters and major calamities caused by human activity
> Sea and land surveillance

It appears relatively innocent. Now I'm so concentrated that I am oblivious to everything around me. The place was deserted when I sat down with my laptop, now I suddenly notice there are people all around me. A few yards away there is a long queue of passengers waiting to board a Widerøe flight to Kirkenes. Fortunately my flight is leaving later. I see an acquaintance in the crowd, but refrain from attracting his attention. I haven't time to talk to him just now. Outside darkness is starting to fall. The mountains on Kvaløya have turned navy blue in color; the rosy tint from the autumn sun has vanished. I still have a couple of hours before I have to pack my laptop away.

I know now that the U.S. Department of Defense is keen to utilize COSMO-SkyMed. But I don't know that much more about the connection to the U.S. Defense, which in turn may well have a co-operation with the Norwegian Armed Forces. Previously I have seen that the U.S. military intelligence unit NGA has been eager to collaborate with commercial radar satellites. Perhaps there is a link between COSMO-SkyMed and NGA?

---

[126] http://www.dtic.mil/descriptivesum/Y2010/OSD/0605130D8Z.pdf (text search for "COSMO-SkyMed")

I try different word combinations. Then I come upon a press release from NGA that I've looked in on several times earlier. This is the announcement of the co-operation between NGA and commercial radar satellites on the purchase of radar satellite images from the pre-Christmas period 2009.

I already know one contract is connected to Radarsat-2, the other to TerraSar-X. But it emerges that a third totally identical contract is signed with the American corporation Lockheed Martin. That's strange, as there are no American companies that have commercial radar satellites. U.S. authorities have not permitted this for fear of data that can be used in warfare going missing out in cyberspace.

But could there be a co-operation between COSMO-SkyMed and Lockheed Martin? I write in "COSMO-SkyMed" and "Lockheed Martin" in the search box. Bingo! The first document to appear is a press release from COSMO-SkyMed's sales company, e-GEOS. Lockheed Martin – one of the giants in the U.S. arms industry – and e-GEOS have jointly sealed a contract with the NGA to supply images from COSMO-SkyMed for up to 85 million dollars! Thereby all three satellite systems that are embraced by NGA's three contracts before Christmas 2009, Radarsat, TerraSar-X and also COSMO-SkyMed, are using Svalbard. The contracts are worth up to NOK 1.5 billion.

Mention should be made of a comment in the NGA press release about the contracts: "The agency's mission is to provide geospatial intelligence(GEOINT), which is the exploitation of satellite or airborne images, to help the war fighters and national decision makers visualize what they need to know. NGA is the nation's eyes."

Of the American military units it isn't just the U.S. intelligence service that makes use of image data from COSMO-SkyMed. The U.S. Navy also use COSMO-SkyMed, together with Radarsat and TerraSar-X. During the last two years the three satellite systems have been used by the U.S. Sixth Fleet, which is comprised of around 40 vessels and submarines, 175 aircraft and 21 000 persons. The U.S. Sixth Fleet is the U.S. Navy's biggest concentration of forces in regard to Europe, which also carries out assignments for NATO. In recent years the fleet has largely operated in the eastern Mediterranean.

Richard J. Schgallis, who was the Commander of the U.S. Sixth Fleet in 2008–2010, wrote in an article of the journal Geospatial Intelligence Forum that: "the U.S. Sixth Fleet has utilized SAR satellites' instruments (that is Radarsat, COSMO-SkyMed and TerraSar-X, author's remark) for fresh surveillance data for support of operational and tactical decisions." According to Bellona at least one of the nuclear-powered submarines in the fleet, the 'USS Hartford', is probably fitted out with nuclear missiles.

I wanted to find a connection between Svalbard and Norwegian warfare in Afghanistan. I haven't succeeded. I've come a long way in determining that the military benefit and use of the system is according to my opinion overwhelmingly in conflict with the Svalbard Treaty. But I find no direct trails that point towards Norwegian soldiers in Afghanistan. Therefore I have to find out more about possible connections, new key words and try different combinations of words.

It emerges that COSMO-SkyMed is a part of the Italian-French satellite co-operation called ORFEO (Optical & Radar Federated Earth Observation). The French contribution is the Pleiades satellite system, which according to the plan is due for launch in 2011 and will capture images with a resolution of less than one meter. Pleiades has applied and received a permit to use Svalsat. The agreement between Italy and France ensures free exchange of data from satellite systems between the two countries.

According to the French space exploration authorities the agreement guarantees that "COSMO-SkyMed and Pleiades ensures that military divisions and intelligence in both countries receive support for their operations". It goes without saying that COSMO-

SkyMed naturally supports French and Italian forces in Afghanistan.

That's why it comes as no surprise that the French arms manufacturer Thales uses data from COSMO-SkyMed together with data from other sources to produce intelligence data for warfare.[127] Thales has a product called MINDS that can accept intelligence data from different types of satellites and surveillance aircraft and handles various data used in warfare. MINDS is used by French Mirage fighter aircraft in Afghanistan.[128]

Norway also uses MINDS, although I am unable to prove that Norway uses MINDS in Afghanistan.[129] It is nonetheless hardly unlikely that data from COSMO-SkyMed isn't downloaded to Norwegian MINDS units for direct use in Norwegian warfare in Afghanistan –given that Norwegian forces are in a difficult situation, and that MINDS would be useful for locating Taliban forces. But I'm unable to prove it.

I keep trying, and combine key words such as the name of the satellite system COSMO-SkyMed with key words for military intelligence activities in Afghanistan like "NATO", "ISAF", "intelligence", "strategic", "tactical" and "mil". It's a slow process. I skim ten or so hits that prove to be totally uninteresting.

A document by Luca Pietranera with the title: "COSMO-SkyMed: Four stories about The Constellation" catches my interest.[130] It turns out to be a PowerPoint presentation of no less than 96 pages that the technical director of the company behind COSMO-SkyMed, e-GEOS, held for American intelligence people

---

[127] www.thaleseurosatory2010.com/appli/.../38_imint_networked_capability.pdf

[128] http://www.dassault-aviation.com/fileadmin/user_upload/redacteur/Defence/2000/Engage_03.pdf

[129] Press Kit, International Paris Air Show 2009

[130] http://usgif.org/system/uploads/1004/original/Luca_Pietranera.pdf

in Washington Thursday 4th March 2010. I start to read. At first it is rather confusing. What the four stories about COSMO-SkyMed are concerned with, are presented as follows:

> Moving garbage sites in North Korea.
> A day in the life of a farmer in Afghanistan.
> Driving in the terrain along a border in the Sahara.
> Handling the relationship between shepherds and fishermen in Somalia.

I try to find out more about the content of the first story – "moving garbage sites in North Korea." The first site shows a black and white satellite image of a landscape titled: "Site monitoring North Korea" – monitoring of an area in North Korea. There is a place name on the map that is illegible in normal showing of the page. I enlarge the image to twice its size, and am certain I can read the word – Yongbyon. I Google Yongbyon and a link to an article from the Washington Post of 4th October 2010 shows up, which informs there are indications of major activity at the North Korean nuclear plant Yongbyon. A satellite image from the company DigitalGlobe shows a river that runs through the area, formations I recognize from the image captured by COSMO-SkyMed.

The next page of the presentation is a satellite image taken by the commercial satellite company WorldView that shows an excavator on the riverbank in North Korea. WorldView uses Kongsberg Satellite Services' ground stations in Antarctica and Tromsø. Clearly this is of interest to South Korean, American or other intelligence services that are customers. The next page of the presentation shows SAR-satellites (probably COSMO-SkyMed, TerraSar-X and Radarsat-2) proof of activity on the riverbank in two places in the period 25th May to 19th June 2009.

The satellite image on the next page is obviously the actual nuclear plant. The heading is "Flat area near the power station", and there is an arrow pointing toward a marked quadrangular, empty area. The presentation shows 16 satellite images of the flat area taken by COSMO-SkyMed from June to October 2009. The images show constant shifting of objects – without mention of

109

what kinds of objects. What is clearly evident is that the purpose of using COSMO-SkyMed in this connection is to reveal North Korea's ability to produce nuclear arms, which could be used in a missile attack against South Korea or the United States.

Luca Pietranera proceeds with his presentation: "Use of SAR for intelligence" is the heading of the next image. Here it is stated that radar satellites can be a good alternative to traditional satellites that take images with sunlight in order to gather new information. He has already shown that with the first example. The information can be to map movement in an area, to decide what type of activity is taking place and to identify hostile targets for attack. It emerges that all types of changes in satellite images taken consecutively are key information.

My jaw drops at the next presentation image. The title: "Northern Afghanistan area". Followed by:

Pilot project in co-operation with the Norwegian Armed Forces
First six images collected between 29th December 2009 and 10th January 2010

The Italian company e-GEOS is using COSMO-SkyMed in a co-operation with the Norwegian Armed Forces to produce intelligence images in North Afghanistan. The first data is downloaded in the period 29th December 2009 to 10th January 2010. Clearly this is the other story Luca Pietranera wishes to present to the American intelligence people in Washington.

The story isn't just about Afghan farmers. I understand that much immediately. Satellite images from different dates are place together. Changes in sections of areas appear as contrast colors.

One example is images of an airfield where there is one known runway and potentially a second. The composite satellite images with contrast colors denoting changes show there was considerable activity on runway number two in the period 1st to 9th

January. In 24 hours 9th to 10th January, there was activity on runway number one, but not on runway number two.

e-GEOS and the Norwegian Armed Forces also use satellite images to monitor traffic on the roads in the region. The satellite data is used to produce composite images that show which roads are used and at what times. The white roads in the mountain landscape were not used in the period 1st to 9th January. The black roads were not used in the period 1st to 10th January. The red roads were used 1st to 9th January, but not the 10th.

The story is supposed to be about a day in the life of an Afghan farmer. What is the connection here? For starters, a composite satellite image with contrast colors for changes taken of an agricultural area showing which fields are ploughed on which days. No one can tell me that farming goals are the main purpose of a co-operation between the Norwegian Armed Forces and COSMO-SkyMed. But this is one way to form an image of activity in the area, amongst others relating to Taliban forces.

The Norwegian forces are stationed in North Afghanistan, and we know the security situation is challenging. COSMO-SkyMed offers some of the most advanced technology in satellite intelligence available in the world today, used against both North Korea and Iran. COSMO-SkyMed produces military intelligence data in co-operation with the Norwegian Armed Forces concerning roads, airfields and other important infrastructure in North Afghanistan.

I find it even more overwhelmingly likely that a satellite system that is controlled from and downloads data on Svalbard is used to actively support Norwegian warfare in Afghanistan. The good intention is to safeguard Norwegian lives in a war, but it isn't in line with Norwegian commitments in the Svalbard Treaty.

I have a sneaking suspicion that the Assistant Governor Lars Fause does not have the full overview of what the satellite systems on Svalbard are used for.

Whether the government has this, I won't pass comment on. In any case the fact is that the government is eager to have more satellite activity on Svalbard.

The first time I became aware of this was when Prime Minister Jens Stoltenberg, fronting half the government presented his northern region strategy in Tromsø 1st December 2006. The government promised to make the northern regions into Norway's most important strategic area for investment. What we often hear in regard to northern region policy is increased co-operation with Russia, everything from removal of Russian nuclear submarines to health, culture and oil and gas in the Barents Sea. That increased space activity in the north is an important part of the government's northern region investment, rates very little mention.

The cover of the pamphlet with the plan that was presented in Tromsø was decorated with North Norwegian motifs such as Saami people in traditional costume and an open fishing boat battling its way through high seas, but also a motif that startles me; a large satellite dish. The explanation was investment in outer space activity, among others on Svalbard, was one of the few concrete initiatives offered by the government. In every State Budget since then money for space activities on Svalbard has been regarded as a vital part of the government's northern region policy. Maybe it isn't all that strange that the Russians are still skeptical about Norwegian Svalbard policy?

I log out and start to gather up my papers. The flight to Vadsø is due to take off soon. There was little or nothing in the applications from the Norwegian Space Centre to the NPT on military use of the German Rapid Eye and Italian COSMO-SkyMed. They had all the appearance of innocent affairs. However after a few hours with open sources, and I know this is not the case.

"If Svalsat is contributing to Norwegian warfare in Afghanistan, it is a breach of the Svalbard Treaty," were the words of the Assistant Governor.

112

I think the connection is obvious enough. Back home in Vadsø I receive confirmation in an e-mail from the NDRE that the Norwegian Armed Forces and NATO have a co-operation with the Italian company e-GEOS on satellite images from Afghanistan, without anyone stating in concrete terms how the images are used.

Chapter 9
New Norwegian satellite station in Antarctica

Director Jan-Gunnar Winther of the Norwegian Polar Institute heads toward one of several large pictures on the wall of his office in Tromsø:

"Come over here. Take a look at this".

The 48year old director with a doctorate has an office on the top floor of the new Framsenteret (the Fram Centre) – complete with a tidy, dark-stained conference table and panorama windows looking out over boat traffic in the Tromsø sound.

"Come here. It's really neat. It's a satellite image of Troll in Antarctica."

He studies the image in complete silence. The satellite image on the wall leaves me open-mouthed: A high definition image of dark house roofs and round white domes spread round in a rocky, naked, Arctic landscape. This is the so-called Troll research station in Antarctica.

In one corner I see the firm name DigitalGlobe. The American satellite company is able to capture images with better than half a meter's resolution.[131] The satellite company can deliver images of a definition unparalleled anywhere else in the world. American military intelligence has therefore secured full control with the best images.[132] According to the Antarctic Treaty there is a total ban on military activity in Antarctica. According to the international agreement the continent shall "be used exclusively for peaceful purposes".

---

[131] http://www.digitalglobe.com/index.php/88/WorldView-2
[132] http://www.satimagingcorp.com/satellite-sensors/worldview-2.html

We both stand there admiring the picture. The unfamiliar perspective. The details. Captured from around seven kilometers above the earth's surface.

"The picture was a gift," said Winther.

The Norwegian Polar Institute runs and operates Troll. DigitalGlobe is one of the satellite companies that use Troll to control and download data from their satellites.

A quite different picture hangs alongside. It is an old black and white image that has been touched up and enlarged. A Polar huntsman posing in heavy leather trousers and leather jacket with a large fur cap covering his head. With both hands in long, thick mittens he holds a rifle diagonally in front of him. He looks straight at me with a proud gaze.

It makes me think that this huntsman perhaps symbolizes what we would rather perceive as characteristic of Norwegian polar traditions and values – the stalwart Norwegian that tackles all manner of challenges. Norwegians and Norway as a nation that leads the way when it comes to tackling a tough climate, researching and exploiting resources in Polar regions. We have national heroes the likes of Fritjof Nansen, Roald Amundsen and Børge Ousland. Jan-Gunnar Winther has met with USA's Secretary of State Hillary Clinton and utilized data on changes in ice conditions in Polar regions in discussions on global climate changes. But something doesn't seem quite right here? Is Norwegian satellite activity gone completely off the rails? Does Norway change its hat to suit the occasion?

In order to understand the satellite industry's interest in Antarctica it can be an idea to try looking at the earth from a distance. As we all know, the earth turns around its own axis in the course of a full day, or 24 hours. By setting a satellite on a fixed course around the North and South Poles it is then possible to gain images of all sections of the planet in the space of a full day. That is why most earth observation satellites travel in a Polar orbit.

115

Kongsberg Satellite Services, KSAT, has from its tender start in 1997 experienced growth the stuff of fairy tales for its control and downloading station for Polar satellites on Svalbard. The reason being that thanks to the station's proximity to the North Pole it can communicate with satellites in all of the 14 orbits these complete around the earth in the course of a 24-hour cycle.

But Kongsberg Satellite Services had higher ambitions. It takes just under two hours for a satellite to go around the earth, and normally the satellite could not download its data to Svalsat when it is out of sight. A satellite station at the other Pole, the South Pole, would result in the satellite being able to download information twice in the course of a single orbit around the earth. The data would then be at the most one hour old before reaching receivers. No other company in the world could offer this. This was the so-called Pole-to-Pole concept.

Industry founder Rolf Skår burned heart and soul for the idea and once again played a key role in the process. He had stepped into the breach to campaign for a large satellite station on Svalbard, despite plenty of skepticism. Skår had enormous faith in building a similar establishment on the opposite side of the earth. But what about consideration to Norway's commitments stipulated in the Antarctic Treaty? The Antarctic Treaty has even stricter formulations against military activity than the Svalbard Treaty. The Antarctic Treaty states that the continent shall be used "exclusively for peaceful purposes". I had asked Skår the same thing when we met at the café in Lillestrøm in the autumn of 2010, and was served the following ambiguous reply: "We were in a competitive situation. If we hadn't taken advantage of this, others would take our place."

At the same time as Kongsberg busied itself with its plans for a satellite station in Antarctica, Jan-Gunnar Winther had already had a number of research sojourns on the world's southernmost continent. The Norwegian Polar Institute was a major driving force in increasing Norwegian activity in Antarctica. In January 2003 the Minister of the Environment Børge Brende was the first Norwegian cabinet minister to visit Antarctica. Both research and political arguments were used so that Norway could have its first year-round base in Antarctica, and the same year Brende (in his capacity as Minister of the Environment) decided to build a year-round station.[133] Two years later Her Royal Highness, Queen Sonja of Norway, opened it with pomp and ceremony.

The first continual activity was that opened by Prime Minister Jens Stoltenberg in January 2008. This was the TrollSat satellite station, owned by Kongsberg Satellite Services, KSAT.[134] TrollSat was established in connection with the Troll research base and was run and is still operated by staff there. The antenna system controls and downloads signals from satellites that orbit over the South Pole.

Thus Kongsberg is able to guarantee that satellite data conveyed to customers is no more than one hour old, as opposed to maximum two hours when using just Tromsø and Svalbard. The company intends to offer all its customers the opportunity use TrollSat. In the space of a few short years Kongsberg Satellite Services has realized its unique Pole-to-Pole concept with solid political support. Now, how was that possible?

We take a giant leap across the globe to the foot of the Øksfjordjøkel glacier in Finnmark County. August 2010, Jan-Gunnar Winther is together with the adventurer Stein P. Aasheim, the former Olympic Nordic skiing champion and woolen knitwear manufacturer Vegard Ulvang and a colleague from the Norwegian Polar Institute, historian Harald Dag Jølle. The four have planned a weekend trip starting from fjord shoreline with a climb to the more than 1000 meter high mountain summit of eternal ice and down again to the shore on the other side.

---

[133] http://www.regjeringen.no/nb/dokumentarkiv/Regjeringen-Bondevik-II/md/Nyheter-og-pressemeldinger/2003/norge_far_helarsstasjon_i_antarktis.html?id=249910

[134] http://romsenter.no/?module=Articles;action=Article.publicShow;ID=50920

Above a clear blue sky, autumn is starting to color the landscape and everyone is in high spirits. Stein P. Aasheim knows Vegard Ulvang well from diverse trips, and teases him for taking so long to get the fire started. Eventually they start the climb up the mountainside with their skis strapped on to their backpacks.

Once up on the plateau the skis are put to good use as they make their way down the other side of the mountain. At the bottom they have arranged with the *Hurtigruten* (Norwegian coastal cruise ship) to detour slightly to pick them up. On board the *M/S NordNorge* Captain Oddleif Engvik treats all four to dinner and drinks, before the evening is concluded with the same four posing in long swimsuits to promote *Hurtigruten's* fashion collection.[135]

Yet another successful training trip has been completed for the planned skiing trip to the South Pole. The plan is to ski the same route that Roald Amundsen took, exactly one hundred years after. The four plan to start from the "Framheim" expedition base in Hvalbukta 19th October 2011, head in over the Ross Ice Shelf, up Axel Heiberg Glacier and travel the last kilometers of the 700 km long trip in to the South Pole in the space of 59 days, mirroring Amundsen's achievement.

The expedition has encountered opposition. Professor Eystein Jansen of the Bjerknes Centre for Climate Research (BCCR) lacks a scientific reason for the expedition, which in total will cost NOK 5 million. This is money provided from public and private sources. The Polar Institute's director, Jan-Gunnar Winther, has publicly defended the payment of his salary during the trip on the grounds that it provides an opportunity to spread important information about Antarctica. The Progressive Party's (Fremskrittsparti) parliamentary representative, Ketil Solvik-Olsen, is of the opinion this is pretty much a "trip for the 'old' boys", and cannot see any value whatsoever for Norwegian taxpayers who will be the ones footing the bill.[136] But that is scarcely enough of an obstacle to stop the trip.

---

[135] http://www.tv2nyhetene.no/magasinet/vegard-ulvang-i-badedrakt-paa-catwalken-3280978.html

The expedition is a part of the Nansen–Amundsen Year 2011, which is a national tribute to the fact it is 150 years since Fridtjof Nansen was born, and 100 years since Roald Amundsen's expedition - as the first expedition - reached the South Pole. The Nansen–Amundsen Year 2011 has full government approval, with responsibility delegated to the Norwegian Polar Institute. Polar traditions still hold a great deal of prestige in Norway.

Jan-Gunnar Winther and the other three won't be the only ones gathered around the Norwegian flag at the South Pole on 14th December 2011 – the hundredth anniversary. Norway's most famous Pole explorer, Børge Ousland, has plans to reach the South Pole with a group of Norwegian leaders of trade and industry via a shorter route. In his New Year's speech for 2011 Prime Minister Jens Stoltenberg disclosed he was also going to the South Pole. So were Liv Arnesen, Asle T. Johansen and Steffen Dahl planning to travel together with others or alone in different routes to the South Pole on this historic day?

In addition there were the foreign tributes. British soldiers with experience from Afghanistan would be heading there. The same applied to the former top Austrian alpine skier Hermann Mayer, who would be competing against a German team to get to the Pole first. A total of at least twelve Norwegian and foreign expeditions of various types were to participate.[137]

In Norwegian history it is also the day that Roald Amundsen planted the Norwegian flag on the South Pole; a red-letter day. The news broke almost three months later, when Amundsen well away from the inland ice sent a telegram home with the following message:

---

[136] http://www.nrk.no/nyheter/distrikt/troms_og_finnmark/1.7355773

[137] http://ut.no/artikkel/1.7456824

"Norway's Flag planted on the South Pole. All well! Roald Amundsen."

The Norwegian Parliament was actually due to discuss a proposal from the budget committee that day. Parliament's President Wollert Konow from the party Frisinnede Venstre stood:

> Colleagues and co-members! We cannot commence the day's work without coming together to express in words the feeling of thankful joy, of admiration and pride that has filled us since we received the message that Roald Amundsen and his men have reached the South Pole and planted the Flag of Norway there. We are uplifted with pure joy and deep gratitude that "Fram" and her brave crew have once more returned unharmed from this dangerous voyage.

The entire House stood and applauded. The South Pole triumph had great significance for creating a separate Norwegian identity in the new Norwegian state.[138] But to the declaration that vast stretches of the continent are Norwegian, is not made there and then. This did not happen until 1939 out of well-founded fears that Nazi Germany had tried to beat Norway to the mark.

The cabinet meeting of 14th January 1939 adopted a bill passing into law that all of Dronning Maud Land – one-sixth of the entire continent – is a part of Norway. This is a gigantic area. Dronning Maud Land is seven times the size of the entire Norwegian mainland. Only Australia has submitted a larger claim than Norway.

On an international level, research and industrial activity are regarded as arguments for states to claim land, and Norway had in the years prior been engaged in whaling and aerial photography for preparing maps. Despite this, Norway did not gain the support of the United States and the Soviet Union, both of which at that time and now claim Antarctica is their area. Germany protested.

---

[138] http://www.polarhistorie.no/filearchive/Amundsen_Levende_historie.pdf

The United Kingdom, France, Argentina, Chile, Australia and New Zealand submit separate claims to land areas in Antarctica.

Since 1961 the Antarctic Treaty has largely ensured political and judicial stability on the continent. The agreement ascertains that the countries' original claims of sovereignty are not relinquished, that the countries cannot make new claims, and that the Antarctica countries shall utilize Antarctica exclusively for peaceful and scientific purposes.[139]

This is an agreement that grew out from successful international research cooperation at the height of the Cold War. It is for that reason understandable that a mainstay of the agreement is that any form whatsoever for military activity is prohibited on the continent. The following is an excerpt from the treaty's introduction:

> Recognizing that it is in the interest of all mankind that Antarctica shall continue forever to be used exclusively for peaceful purposes and shall not become the scene or object of international discord.

This is the first article of the treaty:

> "Antarctica shall be used for peaceful purposes only. There shall be prohibited, inter alia, any measures of a military nature, such as the establishment of military bases and fortifications, the carrying out of military maneuvers, as well as the testing of any type of weapons".

In the sixties, seventies and eighties the level of Norwegian activity in Antarctica varied considerably. Whaling had ceased after Norwegian whalers had in less than an honorable manner taken part in almost eradicating the blue whale, humpback whale, fin whale and Sei whales. The Norwegian authorities maintained participation in the cooperation concerning the Antarctic Treaty ensured Norway's continued claim to Dronning Maud Land and

[139] http://www.npolar.no/no/antarktis/antarktistraktaten.html

other interests in Antarctica. Other nations, such as the former Soviet Union (later Russia) and Japan have throughout the years since the signing of the treaty engaged in large-scale research projects.

At the close of the eighties there were powerful forces eager to start mineral extraction ventures in Antarctica, and the entire Antarctic Treaty was subject to extreme lobbying pressure. Without the treaty Antarctica's fragile political and judicial stability would have been seriously threatened, and an open power struggle to lay claim to the continent could have been the outcome. The Falkland Islands war off the southern coast of Argentina in 1982 between Argentina and the United Kingdom showed that a conflict could easily erupt in the area. The Norwegian Ministry of Foreign Affairs contended Norway should have a new Norwegian research station in Antarctica to better safeguard Norwegian interests.[140]

On 11th January 1990 the 106-metre long Norwegian coastguard icebreaker "Andenes" anchors off the Prinsesse Astrid Coast in Dronning Maud Land, Antarctica, six weeks after the specially fitted navy vessel left Norway. On board is a hired Bell 214B helicopter and an Ecureuil AS 350 B helicopter in addition to two belted track vehicles of the type Hägglunds Bv206, belonging to the Norwegian Army.

One of the main tasks from the Norwegian Polar Institute and the expedition's other participants is to establish Troll – the new Norwegian base in Antarctica. Nestor for Norwegian Antarctic research the last few decades, Olav Orheim of the Norwegian Polar Institute, is leader of the expedition. For Orheim it is important to avoid that the new station gradually disappears under a mountain of snow and ice, as was the case with a previous Norwegian station. The Norwegian-British-Swedish research expedition Maudheim set up its building on ice in Norselfjorden in 1950. The station was only used during the Antarctic summer,

---

[140] Interview with Olav Orheim, previously Director of Norsk Polarinstitutt (The Norwegian Polar Institute)

which ended up - after a few years - under so much snow that it was impossible to dig into the building itself.

The new Norwegian station would therefore be sited in an area that is snow-free in January/February. Preferably also it should be possible to establish an airbase in the area to ease transport to and from the station.

Earlier the expedition leader had together with American colleagues studied Landsat satellite images in order to find a suitable site for the Norwegian station. Orheim had pointed out an area by the mountain range Jutulsessen 300 km from the edge of the sea as his favorite. There they had both snow-free areas and proximity to a large blue ice area that could be utilized as an airbase.

A helicopter takes off from KV "Andenes" to reconnoiter the area 1200 meters above the sea by Jutulsessen. A group of three inspect the area while the weather is mild and calm. The area definitely meets expectations. Expedition leader Olav Orheim is quickly convinced this is the right place. Not since the early sixties has Norway had a permanent research base in Antarctica, and for Orheim the choice of site for the new Norwegian base in Antarctica is an historic moment.[141]

The two helicopters hoist ashore one hundred metric tons of building materials and other equipment before the Norwegian Army's belted track vehicles can begin the last leg of transport. In total the two belted track vehicles cover a distance of 3000 kilometers – a distance longer than from Paris to Moscow. Two weeks after the KV "Andenes" has arrived at Antarctica, the official opening takes place for the Norwegian station in Dronning Maud Land.

At this point in time Rolf Skår had long since been discussing with Olav Orheim about the importance of Norway being able to receive satellite data in both Antarctica and the

---

[141] See previous note

Arctic. Nonetheless time drags on before Troll is put to use for satellite purposes. There is little activity otherwise at the station. It's only in the summer seasons there is some research activity at the station. The Norwegian Polar Institute exerts pressure to have the station operating all year round. A well-used argument is that Norway is the only one of the seven countries with claims to own areas in Antarctica that doesn't have a year-round research station.

Things only get moving after the Minister of the Environment Børge Brende, as the first Norwegian cabinet minister to do so, visits Antarctica in late January/early February 2003 to highlight the Norwegian presence. He arrives in a Russian aircraft from South Africa. The pilot flying the Ilyushin aircraft carrying Brende and company lands on the glacial ice near Troll in minimum visibility. The stormy weather forces the passengers to stay six-seven hours in a large Russian tent out on the blue ice before they can safely continue the minister's programme.

The wild, virgin scenery leaves a powerful impression on Brende, who is a keen hiker at home in the Norwegian mountains. Brende also gets to see the comprehensive research activities that South Africa and other countries are engaged in in Dronning Maud Land. The Minister of the Environment decides after the trip that Troll shall be upgraded to a year-round research station in time for 2005 when Norway would celebrate its 100th jubilee as an independent state.

The year after Brende has become the Minister for Trade and Commerce, and gives his blessing to a cooperation agreement between the Norwegian Polar Institute and the Norwegian Space Centre in regard to Troll. Brende meets up in person for the signing of the agreement, which he calls "pioneering in that it takes care of research interests at the same time as it lays the groundwork for important industrial/commercial activity".[142]

---

[142]

http://www.romsenter.no/?module=Articles;action=Article.publicShow;ID=402 96

The agreement commits the Norwegian Space Centre to get Norwegian Romsenter Eiendom AS to pay for an antenna on Troll that will enable Kongsberg Satellite Services to send data to customers from a planned Kongsberg antenna at Troll. The Polar Institute will only use antenna purchased by Norwegian Romsenter Eiendom for own satellite communication against supplying power and being in charge of the daily operation of the Kongsberg antenna.

Those involved in the work of using Troll for satellite activity, are aware of the political danger of establishing Norwegian satellite activity in Antarctica. The Ministry of Foreign Affairs enters the picture, and it considers whether downloading data from satellites and controlling satellites in Antarctica, might be in conflict with the Antarctic Treaty. Both the United States and Germany have equipment at their research bases in Antarctica to communicate with satellites, but the equipment has far from the same capacity as the planned Norwegian facility. The conclusion of the review is that a Norwegian satellite station is in accordance with all parts of the treaty.[143]

On 12th February 2005, the date of the official opening of Troll as a year-round base, which is to be celebrated with due pomp and ceremony. The Norwegian Air Force flies in a large group of distinguished guests with Queen Sonja at the forefront. Queen Sonja is the first member of the Norwegian royal family to visit the continent. Packed snugly in a heavyweight, dark Polar jacket and a large, red woolen cap pulled down well over her ears, Sonja takes her position in front of the steps to the biggest red container building on Troll, armed with a small piece of paper with catchwords and proceeds to carry out the official inauguration speech.

Down on the graveled slope stands among others the chairman of the Norwegian Parliament's foreign affairs committee, Thorbjørn Jagland, side by side with the Norwegian Minister of the Environment Knut Arild Hareide, the Swedish Minister of the

---

[143] See note 140

Environment Lena Sommestad and other prominent guests – all snug in heavy winter clothing, far from their normal surroundings.

In her speech Queen Sonja stresses Antarctica's significance as the world's biggest and least touched wilderness and the continent's role in providing valuable knowledge about the planet's past and future. Then she lays a ball of ice between three stones as the formal marking of the occasion: The Norwegian year-round station is now officially opened. The ceremony is a pronounced political gesture to show that Norway still has ambitions in Antarctica.

Three weeks later in, in March 2005, Kongsberg Gruppen ASA issues a stock exchange report that the subsidary Kongsberg Satellite Services has signed a contract with the U.S. satellite company Orbimage on the downloading of data and control of the OrbView-5 satellite.

Due to this contract Kongsberg Satellite Services will commence the establishment of TrollSat, which is a new receiver station for satellite data in Antarctica. Providing final approval is given by the Norwegian authorities, TrollSat will be established in connection with the Norwegian research base, which is run by the Norwegian Polar Institute.[144]

OrbView-5 is a cooperation project between the private American company Orbimage and the U.S. military intelligence service NGA.[145] The new satellite shall have the world's best resolution for commercial satellites – 41 centimeters – and the images with highest resolution will be reserved for U.S. military intelligence. U.S. intelligence injects one billion dollars into the project.

---

[144] http://www.kongsberg.com/nb-NO/KOG/News/2005/March/0307EstablishingSatelliteStationAntarctic/

[145] http://www.10.giscafe.com/nbc/articles/view_article.php?section=CorpNews&articleid=145377

As we have already seen, a cooperation had long since been established between the Norwegian Space Centre and the Norwegian Polar Institute – supported by the Minister of Trade and Commerce Børge Brende – to enable Kongsberg Satellite Services to utilize Troll as a satellite station. Kongsberg Satellite Services is owned 50 percent by Norwegian Romsenter Eiendom AS, which is a wholly owned State company under the umbrella of the Ministry of Trade and Commerce, and 50 percent by the Kongsberg Group, of which the Norwegian State via the Ministry of Trade and Commerce owns 50 percent. The Ministry of Trade and Commerce should therefore have good control over activity in Kongsberg Satellite Services.

Signals from executives in the Ministry of Trade and Commerce headed by Cabinet Minister Børge Brende have been more than clear: There is solid political support for the new Norwegian satellite station in Antarctica, whose establishment is owed as a result of a contract in which U.S. military intelligence is heavily involved.

The year after a Russian icebreaker is tied up at quayside just outside the windows of Director Jan-Gunnar Winther's office at the Norwegian Polar Institute in Tromsø. Soon it will set sail from Norway to the edge of the Antarctica ice with the biggest cargo ever of equipment from Norway – including advanced satellite equipment.[146] Most of the over hundred staff that Jan-Gunnar Winther will lead from his office, are connected to diverse scientific research objectives. However the job of controlling and downloading data from satellites will be the initial normal activity for the Norwegian Polar Institute's new Norwegian base on the other side of the planet.

---

[146] http://www.statsbygg.no/Aktuelt/Nyheter/7060/

CHAPTER 10
Military bridgehead on the Continent of Peace

In the mid-seventies a young man was sitting in the shopping precinct South Street Seaport in Lower Manhattan in New York, strumming his guitar to make a living. Matt O'Connell was later to become a key figure in the establishment of the Norwegian Satellite station in the Antarctic. He is now a successful businessman with an annual income of well over NOK ten millions.

The well-spoken and humoristic O'Connell is slim and fit, belying his 57 years. On official occasions he is usually clad in a dark blue suit with a white handkerchief neatly folded in his left breast pocket. He has unwavering and direct eyes, his healthy head of hair combed back from his brow.

There's little in his formative years to indicate a successful career in business. Matt's prime interest is music. After college he earns his living primarily from his guitar and mandolin. He starts studying again, but not economics and technical subjects. Matt studies Latin and Greek, while continuing to nurture his musical interests with a number of groups.

Matt starts studying law, and in the passage of time creates a career for himself as a lawyer in Wall Street in Manhattan. His field is corporate law, working for the bank Crest Advisors LCC, Sony and a number of other companies for the next 20 or so years. This continues until a failed satellite launch turns his career on its head.

On the morning of 21st September 2001, ten days after the attack on the World Trade Center, the satellite Orbview-4 is perched on the top of the launch vehicle Taurus at the Vandenberg Air Force Base in California. Everything's ready for launching the satellite into orbit. The satellite is owned by the company Orbimage and the plan is that it will be able to capture monochrome and color images of a higher quality than that offered by any other satellite operating in the global marketplace. The company has had major financial problems and a successful launch is essential for its future survival.

The launch vehicle carrying Orbview-4 lifts off as planned, but just minutes after liftoff things start to go wrong. The launch vehicle becomes unbalanced, and fails to gain sufficient height to place the satellite in the correct earth orbit. The crew in the control center release Orbview-4 from the launch vehicle. The satellite must gain orbital altitude under its own power, but fails to do so. Gravity wins the tug of war and Orbview-4 crashes into the Indian Ocean.

Immediately after the event Matt O'Connell receives a phone call. He is asked if he will consider leading a financial turnaround operation for the company. The reason behind the approach is that he has contributed on occasions with legal advice and assistance for a number of companies that found themselves in dire financial straits.

After the terrorist attacks on the USA the possession of technology that can observe bad guys from space must be a sound business idea is Matt's first thought,[147] and he accepts the challenge, which he believes will mean a few flights to the head offices in Washington, and will take a month or two.

Ten years later Matt is still at the helm of the company despite the fact that he is still completely green as far as satellite technology is concerned. The company, now called GeoEye, has seen explosive growth and is a hot name on the New York Stock Exchange.

Matt – or Matthew, which is his given name – was by no means wrong in his prediction concerning the Pentagon's appetite satellite data after the terrorist attacks on the USA. The channels

---

[147] http://www.defensemedianetwork.com/stories/eyes-in-the-skies/

were already open prior to the 11th September attacks. It was in the same year that Orbimage had been awarded a contract worth roughly NOK 700 million for the development of new intelligence products. More, much more was to come – particularly after President George W. Bush signed a directive in 2003 that American intelligence was to concentrate on using images from commercial companies in what he called the war on terror. This means that amongst other things all forms of military maps and charts shall be produced on the basis of data gleaned from commercial satellite images. This policy is designed to ensure that American companies will maintain their positions as market leaders in their respective areas and would also secure American jobs.

The three American companies with advanced earth observation satellites, Orbimage, DigitalGlobe and Space Imaging, are all extremely busy during the invasion of Iraq in 2003. The satellites are part of a programme used to detect Iraq's Patriot missiles and air defense systems in the planning and conquering of Kirkuk, as well as to identify minefields along the borders of Iraq and Iran. The Pentagon's appetite for satellite data doesn't exactly diminish.

In March 2004 Orbimage enters into a new contract with the NGA. The contract price is not the particularly large – only NOK 200 million – but the so-called ClearView contract is important because it forms the basis for a longer term and closer relationship between the company and the NGA than previous contracts.[148] The Pentagon uses the ClearView contract to gain control of all new satellite images of Afghanistan.
This is done to enable the USA and the allies to use the material and also to prevent the Taliban from being able to purchase images.

In the same year Orbimage enters into a new and much larger contract with the NGA in a contract programme known as NextView.[149] DigitalGlobe enters into an identical contract, but

[148] http://geoeye.mediaroom.com/index.php?s=43&item=84

Space Imaging does not. Orbimage then acquires Space Imaging and adopts the new name GeoEye. The new contracts provide technical and financial support for the development and construction of even more advanced satellites and secure American intelligence and other defense forces high-resolution satellite images for the coming decade. The contract sum for GeoEye is in the region of NOK three billions. GeoEye and the American intelligence organizations are to co-operate on the construction of a new satellite with resolution down to 41 centimeters, better than any satellite in the global marketplace. The satellite is first named OrbView-5, later renamed Geoeye-1. Just under six months later Kongsberg Satellite Services issues a stock exchange notice about its co-operation with Orbimage, the company that just after this changes its name to GeoEye, in which it is determined that the co-operation will result in the establishment of Trollsat.[150]

In plenty of time prior to the launch of the new American satellite that will be controlled from and downstream data to the Antarctic, Matt O'Connell is at Vandenberg Air Force Base in California together with a number of his closest colleague. There is much at stake, and he is uneasy. Seven years earlier a launch vehicle carrying the company's OrbView-4 had launched from Vandenberg only to fail, and he is well aware that history can repeat itself. The company could once again be plunged into financial difficulties.

It became even more difficult for the CEO to keep his nerves steady when he was told that the launch had been delayed for the second time. The launch was originally scheduled to take place 12 months ago. Constant delays result in that the cash flow from operations is also delayed, resulting in a fall in the company's share price on the New York Stock Exchange.

He has a box of cigars he took with him to celebrate. His wife, Libby, who has been with him since his time as a musician, is

[149] http://geoeye.mediaroom.com/index.php?s=43&item=76

[150] http://www.netfonds.se/quotes/release.php?id=20050307.OBl.15504

by his side. The waiting is nonetheless difficult. Matt changes from a suit to a tracksuit and sports shoes. He's going to take part in competition next week, a triathlon, swimming, cycling and running. He finds that the vigorous exercise helps to allay his nerves ...

At last the new launch date arrives, and Mr. and Mrs. O'Connell take their places to follow the countdown to the launch. Also present are the founders of Google, Sergey Brin and Larry Page. Earlier in the same week GeoEye and Google have announced that Google has purchased the rights to satellite images from Geoeye-1 that are not subject to military restrictions. Google wants the images in connection with the company's location and map and services, Google Earth and Google Maps.

The press release for the launch quotes Matt O'Connell as saying the new satellite will make it easier to enter into co-operative agreements with the Pentagon. During the final nerve-racking minutes prior to the launch Sergey turns to the GeoEye CEO and says: "Well Matt, when will we be getting more of the same type?"

Matt O'Connell turns towards him, replying: "Sergey, I'm just a little distracted right now!"[151]

At precisely 11:50 on 6th September 2008 the launch vehicle for GeoEye lifts from the launch ramp and commences its climb towards the heavens from Vandenberg Air Force Base in California. The first report comes from the ground station in Tromsø, which sends the message that everything is functioning as planned, a tremendous relief for all who have worked for the past four years in designing and constructing the satellite.

"So far everything is going well with the initial tests, the satellite is in its prescribed orbit, and we are looking forward to receiving the first images", says the Vice Director of the NGA, Admiral Robert B. Murret.[152]

---

[151] See note 147

Two days later the first images are published, images of the University area in Kutztown, Pennsylvania, USA. It's easy with nothing more than a standard PC to zoom in to the photograph and see two people playing tennis, pedestrians on a pavement, how traffic is developing at a road junction and to read the advertising billboards at the football stadium.[153]

It's perhaps not so strange that the NGA is almost delirious with enthusiasm after having completed a three-month long evaluation of Geoeye-1. The work is commented on in the NGA's own magazine, Pathfinder. Cyndi Wright, the executive responsible for the implementation of the two NextView contracts that Geoeye-1 is part of, writes that "military units in combat zones had expressed the need for access to easily available, non-confidential high quality images and image-based products in a format they can easily use and process [...] the NextView-programme and the two commercial satellite suppliers, GeoEye and DigitalGlobe, represent a capacity that will meet with and exceed this requirement [...] Geoeye-1 represents a quantum leap with regard to access to commercial satellite images for USA."[154]

One of the most valuable products the NGA uses the new satellite images to make for American forces is a book for American soldiers in Baghdad. The book has high-resolution images of the City on the right hand page and a listing the names of all the streets and buildings on the left.[155]

The NGA emphasizes: Pursuant to the GeoEye and American regulations, military graded information from GeoEye can be shared with our allies, which is not the case with data from American military satellites. Images of nuclear plants and other

152
https://www1.nga.mil/Newsroom/Pathfinder/0606/Pages/AgencyApplaudsLaunchofGEOEYE-1Satellite.aspx
[153] http://www.defensenews.com/story.php?i=3778072
[154] http://www.defensenews.com/story.php?i=3778072
[155] http://www.defensesystems.com/Articles/2009/03/11/NextView-launches-second-satellite.aspx

installations can be distributed to our allies, which is important to the USA in the effort to stop the proliferation of nuclear weapons. The images are also important for the planning of joint combat operations, the operations themselves and evaluating damage from aerial bombardments.

The Norwegian Satellite station in the Antarctic is of prime importance to Geoeye-1. Apart from the station in the Antarctic only two other stations, Tromsø and a station in Alaska are receiving and command stations for Geoeye-1 near the Poles. In addition to the GeoEye stations near the Poles, the company has a receiving and command station at the company's headquarters near Washington.

In the same year that Geoeye-1 is launched – 2008 – Norwegian Prime Minister Jens Stoltenberg visits the Antarctic. There had been a discussion in the Prime Minister's office as to how best celebrate the International Polar Year when the idea of a visit to the Antarctic was born. This had been one of Stoltenberg's childhood dreams, and now it was a reality.

Stoltenberg arrives in Dronning Maud Land in a Hercules aircraft that touches down on the blue ice in perfect weather, with a cloudless blue sky and just a few degrees below zero early on the morning of Saturday 19th January 2008. The Prime Minister says he is in the Antarctic to highlight Norwegian interests, to recognize the work of the Norwegian Polar scientists and researchers in connection with climate challenges and to honor our long and proud Polar traditions. Stoltenberg is first Norwegian Prime Minister to visit the world's southernmost continent.

The Norwegian Prime Minister and his large entourage of journalists, all clad in red and blue winter outer suits with Norwegian flags on the shoulders are billeted in large tents on the ice. Stoltenberg presides over the formal opening of TrollSat later that day by connecting two data carrier cables: "The satellite station is a milestone in environmental monitoring by satellite. It illustrates Norway's unique position in Polar research in that we can now download data both on Svalbard and in Dronning Maud

Land. It is in accordance with Norwegian Polar traditions to utilize the Antarctic for this purpose", says Jens Stoltenberg.[156]

He is asked by a journalist what his intentions for Dronning Maud Land are. "I want to see it preserved as it is. We have to secure and protect this fantastic, pristine nature while at the same time carrying out research. The key to understanding amongst other things climate issues is here. Norway has some of the best Polar researchers in the world – and thus also some of the world's best climate scientists", is Stoltenberg's reply.[157]

He makes no mention of military objectives. So how do the Norwegian authorities deal with the matter of permits for satellite-based activities in the Antarctic?

The first application for a permit for satellite activities in the Antarctic is from Kongsberg Satellite Services to the Norwegian Post and Telecommunications Authority on 16th February 2005 for the satellite OrbView-5, later called Geoeye-1.

According to the application the images from the satellite will amongst other things "be used for charting terrain and for pipe-laying, in the planning and development of major plant construction, for forestry and agricultural objectives and travel planning" and that "all data is commercially available". The fact is that the American military intelligence service paid in the region of NOK two billions of the total cost of the satellite of just over NOK three billions.[158] The NGA doesn't hand out billions to get nothing in return. American regulations do not permit the sale of the best images on the open market.[159]

---

[156] http://www.norge.se/News_and_events/Samfunn-og-Politikk/Trollsat_no/

[157] http://www.nrk.no/nyheter/1.4574569

[158] http://www.spacenews.com/earth_observation/09111-geoeye-reports-sharply-higher-earnings.html

[159] http://launch.geoeye.com/LaunchSite/about/faq.aspx

The Norwegian Post and Telecommunications Authority doesn't take long to issue a permit for OrbView-5/Geoeye-1 to download data in the Antarctic as well as permission to transmit the download data via fixed equatorial satellites. In the permit – which for some strange reason is written in English – it says that Orbimage has no activities in military operations or links to military operations or systems. There is good reason to question these formulations.

After processing the application for OrbView-5/Geoeye-1, the Norwegian Post and Telecommunications Authority arrives at the conclusion that pursuant to the currently applicable Norwegian laws and regulations, it's actually not necessary to have a permit in order to download data in the Antarctic. The reason for this is that no dedicated legislation or rules have been prepared for satellite activities in the Antarctic to accommodate the Antarctic Treaty, as was the case with satellite-related activities on Svalbard to accommodate the Svalbard Treaty. Even today no such regulations have been penned for the Antarctic, and neither have the regulations for Svalbard been amended to also encompass the Antarctic. The Norwegian Post and Telecommunications Authority has been requesting that this be done for many years.[160]

There is nonetheless a requirement for a permit if one is to transmit signals to a satellite from Antarctica. The Norwegian Post and Telecommunications Authority is of the opinion that the Antarctic Treaty does not impose stricter limitations on military activities on the continent than the Svalbard Treaty does for Svalbard, and in 2008 proposes that TrollSat should, for the sake of simplicity, be given a permit to transmit signals to all satellites that have been given permits to use Svalbard. The Ministry of Justice and Public Security reacts strongly to this. In a letter to the Norwegian Post and Telecommunications Authority the Ministry of Justice and Public Security compares the texts of the two documents against each other. First; the Antarctic Treaty Article 1:

---

[160] Interview with Head of Department Geir Jan Sundal i Post- og teletilsynet, (The Norwegian Post and Telecommunications Authority) November 2010

Antarctica shall be used for peaceful purposes only. There shall be prohibited, *inter alia*, any measure of a military nature, such as the establishment of military bases and fortifications, the carrying out of military maneuvers, as well as the testing of any type of weapon.

In comparison, the Svalbard Treaty's Article 9 says:

Norway [undertakes] not to create nor to allow the establishment of any naval base in the territories specified in Article 1 and not to construct any fortification in the said territories, which may never be used for warlike purposes.

The following is the conclusion drawn by the Ministry of Justice and Public Security from its comparison of the Antarctic Treaty and the Svalbard Treaty:

It can be seen from the comparison of the above-quoted Articles that the Antarctic Treaty, to a higher degree than the Svalbard Treaty stipulates that the area covered by the Treaty shall be non-military. It is thus our opinion that the results of evaluations of the Svalbard Treaty's Article 9 cannot be automatically used as the basis for an evaluation of whether a measure or action is in accordance with the Antarctic Treaty, cf. Article 1 of the said treaty.

The Ministry of Foreign Affairs is responsible for ensuring that Norway adheres to the Antarctic Treaty, and a meeting is called for 8th January 2008 at the Ministry of Foreign Affairs to discuss the case. Representatives from the Ministry of Justice and Public Security, the Ministry of Transport and Communications, the Norwegian Post and Telecommunications Authority, The Norwegian Space Centre and Kongsberg Satellite Services are in attendance. Kongsberg Satellite Services distributes a memo that the company feels will shed light on the matter. Of special interest is the first part of the paragraph "Military and civil systems":

Military systems, and data from civil (commercial) systems that is used for military purposes and objectives, seldom make use of commercial earth stations. This because the transmission of data must be secure from the satellite and to the military operations room where the information is to be used. It is not considered to be safe and secure to allow military data that is for use in public military operations to be transmitted via open channels and general earth stations.

The memo was prepared just after we had seen a massive increase in the military use of Svalsat and not least interest by the military in using TrollSat. The Pentagon increases its priority for the use of commercial satellites through programs such as ClearView, NextView and EnhancedView. For the USA, a country that sets the example for military developments for many other nations, commercial satellites have become a vital and necessary supplement to its own military satellites.

The military is naturally enough concerned about the security of earth stations. It's for this reason that two independent fiber cables have been laid between the Norwegian mainland and Svalbard, and secret security measures have been introduced at Svalsat and TrollSat. TrollSat also has the added security advantage that the station is located six to seven hours by air from the closest airport.

The Ministry of Foreign Affairs has no expertise in satellite activities, and Polar Advisor Karstein Klepsvik, who is responsible for these matters in the Ministry of Foreign Affairs, has a background as a media spokesman and Whaling Commissioner. He is naturally enough very dependent on Kongsberg Satellite Services, the Norwegian Post and Telecommunications Authority, The Norwegian Defense Research Establishment and other external parties' assessments and opinions. Kongsberg makes it clear that they will allow all satellites that use Svalsat to also use TrollSat. There is agreement at the meeting that while awaiting the final regulations dedicated to Norwegian satellite activities in the Antarctic, Kongsberg shall provide regular reports on the development at TrollSat.

On 6th September in the same year ordinary operations of the Norwegian station in Dronning Maud Land commence with the launch of Geoeye-1 from Vandenberg Air Force Base. TrollSat services the satellite regularly by receiving earth observation data and various commands.[161] In one or more orbits the satellite can for example be programmed to first scan a rectangular area covering the whole of the Sognefjord and part of the surrounding mountain ranges, then a large rectangular agricultural area in the south of France before the satellite scans an area in the Sahara. In the course of a 24-hour period Geoeye-1 can capture images of an area the size of Poland with a resolution down to less than a half-meter and stipulate locations with a deviation of less than three meters.

A few weeks later Kongsberg Satellite Services writes to the Norwegian Post and Telecommunications Authority and confirms the following:

> The establishment of TrollSat is a success. The station is the sole freely available satellite station that can be utilized for the receipt of data from and to control earth observation and meteorological satellites (in the Antarctic, author's note). The establishment of TrollSat has put focus on Norway as a polar nation and clearly illustrates Norway's will to contribute in global environmental monitoring.

It's not only the half-military company GeoEye that wants to use TrollSat. DigitalGlobe, the other major American earth observation company is also keen. It's no exaggeration to describe the company's latest creation WorldView-1 as first and foremost a satellite for American intelligence. As is the case with Geoeye-1, WorldView-1 forms part of NextView, the National Geospatial-Intelligence Agency's (NGA) investments in commercial satellites. NGA imposes technical requirements for DigitalGlobe, in return for which they provide funding and commit to buying images.

---

[161] http://www.djupdal.org/asbjoern/antarktis/?p=53

DigitalGlobe must obtain the remaining capital from private investors.

Just after the launch of WorldView-1 from Vandenberg Air Force Base in September 2007 the NGA releases the following announcement to the media: "The new WorldView images will provide the basis for an ever broader programme for the whole of the diverse community of GEOINT analysts (GEOINT: Intelligence linked to locations, author's note), military forces and our allies".

DigitalGlobe makes no effort to conceal the fact that the company is on import to American and other nations' military forces. On the company's Internet pages one finds a detailed overview of the products the company can offer to intelligence and other military units, including information on the contributions WorldView-1 can make.

Satellite data can for example be utilized by air combat forces to differentiate between apparently identical aircraft at ground level and to identify aircraft hangers with especially reinforced construction and the construction of new sub-terrain plant. Satellite images can provide naval forces with information about vessel types, construction, weapons systems, antennae and anchoring systems. Ground forces can retrieve detailed information about enemy movements, for example images of armored personnel carriers and tanks.

The Pentagon is extremely satisfied with the role of WorldView-1 and the other satellites owned by DigitalGlobe and GeoEye that supply data to the American armed forces. Secretary of State for the Pentagon between 2007 and 2010, James R. Clapper, was asked in an interview with Geospatial Intelligence Forum what he could say publicly about the most important and exciting development in the use of GEOINT Technology for the American armed forces. Here is his answer:

The first thing that comes to mind is not really a GEOINT technology, per se, but rather an application of GEOINT collection— the availability of high-resolution, unclassified

140

commercial imagery to the soldier in the field. Because it is so readily usable, and can be shared with coalition partners and with state and local governments, it continues to grow as the preferred source in many operational environments. The launch of World- View-1, the pending launch of GeoEye-1, and NGA's strong partnership with commercial data providers will continue to help ensure we provide the right information, to the right people, at the right time, and in the format and at the classification level that best enables mission success.[162]

These words do not come from a nobody. On 5th June 2010 President Barack Obama walks out onto the Whitehouse lawn together with none other than James R. Clapper. In a brief announcement the President announces that Clapper is the President's choice to lead the 16 intelligence organizations in the USA.

Clapper is given responsibility for the implementation of Barack Obama's plan for the next generation of American intelligence satellites, where commercial satellites will also play a key role. The plan is called *two-plus-two*, because two new military intelligence gathering satellites are to be developed and built to replace the current military satellites, while at the same time two new commercial satellites are to be developed and built. The new commercial satellites will provide images with resolution down to 25 centimeters. The images will be updated on a 24-hour continuous basis and will be made available to military leaders and soldiers in combat without delay.[163]

By 6th August 2010 it's clear that DigitalGlobe and GeoEye have been awarded major new contracts with the National Geospatial-Intelligence Agency. The two contracts have a framework of roughly NOK 40 billion.[164] In 2010 DigitalGlobe

---

[162] http://www.geospatial-intelligence-forum.com/mgt-home/143-mgt-2007-volume-5-issue-6/1263-qaa-james-r-clapper-jr.html
[163] http://www.thespacereview.com/article/1516/1

[164] http://www.euroconsult-ec.com/news/euroconsult-in-the-news-34-3/197.html

141

earned 78 percent of its revenues from intelligence and other military units. A large chunk of this, 62 percent, came from the NGA.[165] Both companies are rising stars on the New York Stock Exchange and achieve their best share prices to date.

Naturally enough, major contracts also mean good times for sub-suppliers. On 20th December 2010 Kongsberg Satellite Services signs its biggest contract thus far for a Norwegian earth station with DigitalGlobe. The contract has a framework of NOK 1.1 billion. The satellites will also be controlled from Tromsø, making the city an even more obvious target for bombing and attack in military conflicts or a terrorist attack.

As is the case with Tromsø and Svalbard, security arrangements have also been put in place around TrollSat in the Antarctic. Daily life at the outpost Troll and TrollSat is nonetheless very peaceful and quiet. One of the few who spend the winter months at the Norwegian "research station" has as his main task looking after the antennas. The antennas are controlled mainly from Tromsø, but it happens that the operator in Tromsø calls the supervisor in Dronning Maud Land for assistance when problems arise. Apart from this, it's necessary that all moving parts are greased and lubricated at regular intervals.

There is an ever-increasing number of antennas and increased traffic to manage at TrollSat. Both Radarsat-satellites have been using the station for some time, as have the German TerraSar-X and Tandem-X satellites. The American WorldView-2 uploading images with last than one half-meter resolution. The Pentagon has ruled that the most detailed images shall have a resolution of minimum one half-meter for sales to the international market. In 2013 WorldView-3 will enter into orbit and commence uploading images to TrollSat. The resolution of these images will be 25 centimeters. During the course of the same year GeoEye has plans to launch its new satellite, Geoeye-2, with the same

---

[165] http://www.faqs.org/sec-filings/110228/DIGITALGLOBE-INC_10-K/

resolution. This will also use TrollSat. Kongsberg's wish is that all satellites that use Svalsat will also use TrollSat.

Norway is alone on having an earth station in the Antarctic that operates on normal commercial terms, and the international satellite industry has formed a queue to use its services. Kongsberg Satellite Services has already commenced work on the construction of five or six new antenna, even though no Norwegian regulations have yet been put in place for satellite activities in the Antarctic. The work has been ongoing since 2007.

At the same time we have a Norwegian Prime Minister who is still full of enthusiasm about Norwegian activities on the other side of the world. In the autumn of 2010 he wrote the following personal message to the staff at the station:

> Norwegian Polar activity is something I am very proud of. It is both important and the right thing that Norway is present and clearly visible on this gigantic continent that is the Antarctic. The Troll Station is the spearhead of Norwegian research in the Antarctic. It makes it possible for Norway to participate to the full in international Polar and climate research. In 2008 I had the honor of opening the Satellite Station TrollSat. The station is a milestone for effective environmental monitoring from satellites and gives better and faster access to amongst other vital climate, environmental and weather data.[166]

Matt O'Connell of GeoEye is enjoying good days. During his first two years in the satellite business he saw major deficits, and he had to go on many trips to his headquarters in Washington and stay at the cheap Holiday Inn. It's all changed now, all indices are pointing straight up, and Matt has no plans to take up his career as a lawyer again. He has sold his house in New York and moved to Washington.

---

[166] http://brage.bibsys.no/npolar/bitstream/URN:NBN:no-bibsys_brage_14645/1/Trollposten2010-3.pdf

"We are hiring people like it's going out of fashion. Being in the satellite business right now is fantastic", is O'Connell's comment.[167]

He was 100 % correct in his predictions about developments in earth surveillance. Earnings in the companies increased by 18 percent in 2009 to roughly NOK two billions or USD 320 million. 80 percent of revenues came from America military intelligence and other military units in the USA and other countries.

Both Matt and others in the satellite branch are of the opinion that the time has passed when ever-improving resolution in itself is the decisive factor in winning the fight for clients. GeoEye recently acquired Spadac, a company that specializes in analyzing intelligence images for the Pentagon.

A key premise for success is being able to offer fresh data. GeoEye was the first company that utilized KSAT's pole-to-pole-concept, the sole method of obtaining date from the same satellite twice a day from the same company. GeoEye plans that the new satellite, Geoeye-2, which is part of Obama's *two-plus-two*-plan, shall be controlled from and will upload data to TrollSat. Hot-off-the-press and processed information directly to soldiers in the front line and units in combat zones are important features of developments in the branch according to O'Connell: "I find network based systems exciting, information can be placed directly in the hands of soldiers engaged in combat. We are trying to satisfy this requirement from the intelligence service and others by developing network-based information systems. This will assist our soldiers in combat and intelligence - and emergency aid personnel to make quick and correct decisions."[168]

O'Connell became a star in the American business world after the initial contract with Kongsberg laid the foundations for

---

[167] http://www.upi.com/Science_News/2010/07/01/Satellite-images-of-Earth-a-hot-commodity/UPI-38571278007642/
[168] http://geointv.com/archive/geointv-2010-intv-matt-oconnell/

the establishment of TrollSat. He has received a number of awards and prizes, and in 2010 the American business magazine FORTUNE named the company he runs as one of the 100 fastest growing companies in the USA, Share price growth for GeoEye has not been less than 15 percent for the last three years.

Matt's income in 2009 was 435 000 dollars plus a performance bonus of 200 000 dollars. Dividends from his stake in the company earned him another 270 000 dollar and non-share related stimulation initiatives yet another 431 000 dollar. A pot of 50 000 dollar was specified as "other imbursements". The sum of this, what the Americans "compensation" gave a total of over 1.6 million dollars, or 10 million kroner at the current exchange rate. [169]

It's easy to see that developments in technology and military interests encourage strong money interests to push hard to use the Norwegian plants near the two Poles. But it's extremely doubtful that activities such as these are in line with 'Proud Norwegian Polar Traditions' and the international commitments and obligations Norway has signed up to.

---

[169] http://people.forbes.com/profile/matthew-m-o-connell-j-d-/36609

Chapter 11
Norwegian support for EU's militarization

Just before 9 am on Thursday 21ˢᵗ January 2010 the Minister of Trade and Commerce Trond Giske is in his seat at the Parliamentary European Committee, which consists of representatives for Parliament's Foreign Affairs and Defense Committee as well as members of Parliament's EFTA/EEA (European Economic Area) delegation. Norway's Minister of Foreign Affairs Jonas Gahr Støre also attends. The European Committee has closed meetings.

Today Trond Giske intends to inform Parliament about Norway's satellite cooperation with the EU. Giske is proud of Norway's space exploration activities, and draws attention to the effort made with the Galileo satellite system, Europe's largest infrastructure initiative and one of Europe's most ambitious industrial projects. The goal is to make Galileo into a navigation system that is more precise than the American GPS system, as the industry has seen this as an opportunity to capture market shares in a growing market. The principle for Galileo and other navigation systems is that by knowing the distance from one point to at least three satellites, you can find out your exact location. Giske maintains Galileo plays an important role in creating bonds between Norway and the EU: "For our part this brings us closer to the EU in that we participate wholeheartedly in this. We have key companies that are well positioned to supply Galileo and develop products based on Galileo."[170]

At this point in time Norway has committed to inject Galileo with half a billion Norwegian kroner. Nonetheless Giske is ready to give much, much more. He contends the cooperation between Norway and the EU must be extended to a more binding

---

[170] Minutes subsequently published: http://www.stortinget.no/no/Saker-og-publikasjoner/Publikasjoner/Referater/Europautvalget/2009-2010/100121/

cooperation on another major satellite project, Global Monitoring for Environment and Security, GMES. "Galileo can actually form the mal or model for our participation in the EU's next major investment in space exploration, GMES, which is a programme between the EU and the European space exploration organization, and which focuses mostly on environmental monitoring and public security," said Giske.

Norway has supported Galileo/GMES for a number of years with funding through the EU's so-called framework programme for research and development.

No one in Parliament's European Committee asks about the satellite system's military significance. No questions or remarks are connected to any international security-political consequences of the satellite cooperation.

An official report from 2006 had a totally different perspective on Galileo. The report *"Når sikkerheten er viktigst"* ("When security takes precedence"), produced on commission from the Ministry of Justice and Public Security, has a paragraph called "What is Galileo?" accompanied by the following explanation:

> Galileo is a European initiative to establish a new global system for satellite navigation. The Galileo structure is the first joint strategic European common structure. The navigation system must thus be seen as a crucial strategic material to, and facilitator for, the common European defense and security policy.[171]

Neither is the other of the EU's two major satellite projects a purely civilian project. As is obvious from the name, Global Monitoring for Environment and Security, security is one of the two principal tasks. This is also apparent in official documents from the European Commission (EC) that GMES has both civilian and military tasks, including a unanimous pronouncement from the

[171] http://www.regjeringen.no/nb/dep/jd/dok/nouer/2006/nou-2006-6.html?id=157408

EC on 26th September 2008, to which Norway has also lent its support.[172] GMES will be an important military global intelligence instrument. Plans have been laid and decided to some extent that both GMES and Galileo will utilize Norwegian ground stations on Svalbard and in Antarctica, which I will come back to later in this book.

Galileo and GMES are thus part of a joint European defense and security policy, a policy that the EU has gradually built up since the signing of the Maastricht Treaty in 1992.[173]

The EU has its first military foreign operation in Macedonia in March 2003, and in July 2004 EU foreign affairs ministers approve the establishment of the European Defense Agency, which receives the key task of chiseling out a common defense policy. Progress continues, and the Lisbon Treaty from 2007 opts for a common security and defense policy, and to a large extent also a shared defense system.[174]

In order to prevent U.S. dominance France in particular advocates for a dynamic joint European outer space policy. This was clearly apparent in President Jacques Chirac's speech during the 40th jubilee for the French National Centre for Space Exploration in December 2001: "The United States spends six times as much public money on the space sector as Europe does. If we don't do anything about it, we can be doubly sure we will end up first as technical and scientific tenants, and subsequently as industrial and financial tenants", he said.[175]

France is out in front where European space exploration development is concerned – for both civilian and military

---

[172]

http://www.consilium.europa.eu/ueDocs/cms_Data/docs/pressData/en/intm/103050.pdf

[173] Frank Slijper, *From Venus to Mars. The European Union's steps towards the militarization of space,* Transnational Institute
[174] See previous note
[175] http://news.bbc.co.uk/2/hi/europe/1718125.stm

purposes. As the first nation in Europe to do so, France launches its own satellite on 22nd February 1986. It is an earth observation satellite with a resolution of 10 meters – far better than the American Landsat satellites.

This is followed by the launches of four of the so-called Spot satellites, which capture increasingly detailed images of the planet. The images are also sold on the international market, for instance U.S. forces in Iraq and Afghanistan have benefited from the images. A good cooperating relationship is developed between the French space exploration organization CNES and the Norwegian Space Centre, and Spot has utilized both Svalsat and the DORIS station at Ny-Ålesund.[176] DORIS is a worldwide network of ground stations that transmit signals to satellites, which includes adjustment of satellite orbits.

France concerns itself for many years with developing a military cooperation on satellite activity with other European countries – partially through the European space exploration organization ESA, partially through the EU and partially through direct agreements with other countries.

ORFEO is an agreement between France and Italy from 2001 concerning new satellites and exchange of images: Italy commits to establishing a military-civilian ground observation system with a resolution of down to one meter, COSMO-SkyMed, and exchanging the data with. In return France gives Italy images from a new satellite, Pleiades, and also images from Spot satellites.[177]

Four COSMO-SkyMed satellites are now circling the earth, while the first Pleiades satellite is planned for launching in 2011. Kongsberg Satellite Services has long since obtained permits to download data from both satellite systems at Svalsat.

---

[176] Permits Post- og teletilsynet (The Norwegian Post and Telecommunications Authority)

[177] http://smsc.cnes.fr/PLEIADES/GP_organisation.htm

MUSIS is an agreement between France, Germany, Spain, Belgium and Greece dating from November 2008. The difference here is that this is a solely military co-operation. The following is an excerpt from a press release issued by the French defense ministry:

> Images from space are of decisive significance for enabling Europe to have independent intelligence and subsequently making own political choices. The accomplishment of MUSIS will therefore be an important step toward building up a European defense capacity.[178]

The new satellite systems will consolidate on already existing or developed systems such as the Italian COSMO-SkyMed, French Pleiades and German SAR-Lupe. Germany started later than France with developing its spy satellites, but invested heavily from Day One.

The first of five satellites in Germany's first officially declared military intelligence system, SAR-Lupe, is launched on 19th December 2006 from Plesetsk at Archangel in Russia. SAR-Lupe has received permission to utilize Svalsat in connection with the launch. It later emerges that the German armed forces also utilize Svalsat to serve SAR-Lupe after the permit has expired, without this having any consequences whatsoever for Svalsat.[179]

TerraSar-X and Tandem-X are two other new German satellites that utilize Svalsat, and which together with SAR-Lupe provide Germany with its own intelligence capacity.[180] But then relations break down between Berlin and Paris.

WikiLeaks documents from the U.S. Embassy in Berlin reveal that Germany is of the opinion that French participants are

[178] http://www.defense-aerospace.com/article-view/release/99967/europeans-to-develop-next_generation-intel-satellite-network.html
[179] The Governor of Svalbard
[180] http://www.infoterra.de/geo-intelligence

using less than refined methods in competition with the Germans in order to acquire an increasingly larger slice of the world market for satellite technology and sale of data. For instance, France makes a rather special offer to the United Arab Emirates for the purchase of two French satellites. In return, France will send one thousand soldiers to the country with equipment that they will leave behind when the soldiers return home.[181]

Germany decides that in addition to the European cooperation, the country will cooperate with the United States on new intelligence satellites called HIROS – without any form of French involvement. HIROS will enable Germany to be totally independent of France during a crisis situation.[182]

Reports from conversations (later released by WikiLeaks) between representatives from the U.S. Embassy in Berlin, the German intelligence service and German companies involved in HIROS from 2009, provide a unique insight to the planning of HIROS and mechanism of military satellite activity.

HIROS is designed to offer a completely new innovation in commercial satellite surveillance, through being able to deliver three-dimensional (3-D) images without time delays from anywhere on the planet, and by its ability to detect exhaust trails from missile launches with the aid of infrared waves. 3-D images in real time are of huge value to all types of modern warfare. The ability to spot missile launches provides Germany and Europe with fresh capacity to extend the construction and installation of a controversial missile defense arrangement against possible attacks from for example Iran, North Korea or Russia.[183]

This takes place at the same time as ESA starts work on a space-monitoring programme, which is partially financed by Norway. This is a necessary prerequisite for a missile defense

---

[181] http://www.aftenposten.no/spesial/wikileaksdokumenter/article3969917.ece

[182] http://www.aftenposten.no/spesial/wikileaksdokumenter/article3969917.ece

[183] http://www.aftenposten.no/spesial/wikileaksdokumenter/article3969913.ece

system. From November 2010 to February 2011 tests are run where a number of European satellites, radar installations and telescopes participate, including the EISCAT research station at Longyearbyen. The final objective is to be capable of offering monitoring of all objects in space around the clock to military units and other customers.[184]

This is also apparent from the U.S. Embassy reports from Berlin that the American satellite company DigitalGlobe, which in the autumn of 2010 entered into a contract with Kongsberg Satellite Services for up to NOK one billion, writes a Letter of Intent on a cooperation with HIROS. Judging by plans from 2009 the German intelligence service will be responsible for the building of three satellites and DigitalGlobe for three. The American company Lockheed Martin signs a Letter of Intent on the building of ground installations.[185]

The German intelligence service reports indicate that the U.S. intelligence service NGA, will be the biggest customer – "prime client identified".

It is also interesting to note that the entire project will be presented as civilian and officially be used for uncontroversial purposes such as environmental monitoring and to combat changes in the climate (global warming). HIROS has this in common with many other satellite projects such as Landsat, Terra-Aqua and COSMO-SkyMed.

In addition to European countries building up their interests in satellites, the crisis-inflicted countries in the EU are agreed on spending massive sums of money on two major satellite programs, GMES - the programme for monitoring the environment and security and the time, location and navigation system Galileo.

---

[184] see http://www.esa.int/esaMI/SSA/SEMALXFMTGG_0.html and http://www.esa.int/esaCP/SEMC9XOR9HG_Norway_0.html
[185] http://www.aftenposten.no/spesial/wikileaksdokumenter/article3969920.ece

Even one of the United States' closest allies, the United Kingdom, sees the value of independence from GPS, the U.S. military satellite system.

In a given crisis system the United States can disturb or stop the open component of GPS in order to prevent enemies from using the system against the United States. In that way European air and shipping traffic and many segments of the European community would be paralyzed. The USA does not like the European plans, which are becoming more and more concrete just after the turn of the millennium.

December 2001 the U.S. Secretary of Defense Paul Wolfowitz sends a letter to the 15 European defense ministers about Galileo, in which he warns against the plans:

> I am writing to convey my concerns about security ramifications for future NATO operations if the European Union proceeds with Galileo satellite navigation services.[186]

Wolfowitz knows the United States can wipe out or disturb Galileo signals if they should deem this necessary. The problem is that with the planned technical solutions for Galileo, an American attack against Galileo would also destroy the American GPS signals. This puts Wolfowitz in a foul mood.

In the letter the American Secretary of Defense asks the European defense ministers to inform the European transport ministers, who are responsible for the building of Galileo. A few days later EU transport ministers meet in Madrid, and Galileo is on the agenda. No final decision is made then on the building of Galileo. American pressure against the system has increased since 11th September, the day of the terrorist attacks in New York and Washington, admits EU's Minister of Transport, Loyola de Palacio.[187]

---

[186] http://www.spacedaily.com/news/gps-euro-01g.html

[187] See previous note

Some months later, on 26ᵗʰ March 2002, the European transport ministers nonetheless resolve to go ahead with Galileo.

At present only the United States and Russia have 100 % complete and working satellite based navigation systems. China is also keen to achieve this, and in September 2003 the news breaks this country will inject 230 million Euro, or around NOK 2 billion, in Galileo. China is mostly interested in utilizing the Galileo signals for military purposes – Public Regulated Services, PRS. A classified document authored by a State Secretary in the Pentagon, Peter Teets, from August 2004 reveals that the United States is worried. " What will we do 10 years from now when American lives are put at risk because an adversary chooses to leverage the global positioning system or perhaps Galileo constellation to attack American forces with precision?" he wrote.[188]

At a conference in London in the autumn of the same year, American representatives make it clear that the United States will attack the 30 planned Galileo satellites if they are used by a hostile power as for example China.[189]

Galileo is a sensitive point in the relationship between the United States and Europe, and many meetings are held between representatives from both sides of the Atlantic. It transpires that the United States and the EU eventually manage to reach agreement on several cooperative projects between GPS and Galileo. Moreover Kina ultimately withdraws from the cooperation on Galileo. China opts to build its own system.[190] The same applies to Japan and India.[191]

---

[188] http://www.spacedaily.com/news/milspace-04zc.html
[189] See previous note

[190] http://www.chinadaily.com.cn/china/2010-01/16/content_9330209.htm

[191] See
http://www.spacedaily.com/reports/Japan_eyes_building_its_own_GPS_system
_999.html and http://www.strategypage.com/htmw/htspace/20110116.aspx

Technical problems cause constant delays for Galileo, but in the autumn of 2009 progress is made with the allocation of the first satellite contracts. Classified documents from the U.S. Embassy in Berlin, later released by WikiLeaks, have references from a meeting held 2nd October with the chief executive of the German company OHB System, Berry Smutny. The report from the meeting shows that Smutny is convinced French military motives are behind the promotion of Galileo.

> He [Smutny] claims that the EU's desire to develop an alternative to GPS was championed by France after an incident in the war in Kosovo when the United States manipulated GPS to support military operations. Since then, he said, France has actively supported EU investments in the Galileo-system – which Smutny said is due to France's eagerness to ensure their missile control systems' independence of GPS.[192]

According to the same Smutny, Galileo has to purchase American components that provide protection against nuclear attack, as the United States is the only country that has these components, even though France wishes to use equipment exclusively from EU countries. According to Smutny the American components are regarded as arms material by the American authorities and can therefore be denied export licenses.

January 2010 the EU enters into a contract with precisely the German company OHB System and the British company Surrey Satellite Technology Limited on building of the first Galileo satellites in the EU's all-important prestige project. In that Smutny is so closely connected to the project there is good reason to give credit to his evaluations, which indicate that Galileo is without doubt a military system. The Board of Directors of OHB, which is a family-owned company with close ties to the German government, fires Berry Smutny a few days after the Norwegian daily Aftenposten publishes the classified report in January 2011.

---

[192] http://www.aftenposten.no/spesial/wikileaksdokumenter/article3985655.ece

The fact that Galileo is also a military system is confirmed by among others the renowned information base Jane's in London, which is used by the Norwegian Armed Forces and public bodies all over the world.

It has been a long and thorny journey to get the first Galileo contracts signed. The first 14 satellites will not be operative until the year 2014, and it will take many years after that for all the planned 30 satellites to be in full function. It's also been a long-term process to establish Norway's current relationship with Galileo. Since 1994 Norway, through membership in the European Space Exploration Agency ESA, has been a fully active participant.

From 2005 to 2007 Norway leads the effort with Galileo in ESA. This is a period where the work tempo accelerates significantly. In the spring of 2006 Kongsberg Satellite Services enters into an agreement with ESA on the building of a ground station for Galileo on Svalbard.[193] A station building and four antennas are scheduled for erection at Svalsat during the summer. Local companies such as LNS Spitsbergen and Sandmo & Svenkerud again have plenty to do up at Platåberget, and Kongsberg Satellite Services finds it has to increase staffing yet again.

The Norwegian Space Centre participates with direct financial funding, and the contract term is 20 years. Norway promises the EU that the signals between the ground station and Galileo satellites will be shielded against interference and interruptions and that security measures will be put in place at Svalsat to prevent intruders gaining entry. Secret security measures are drawn up for Svalsat.

By Saturday 19th January 2008 all is set for the official occasion to mark commencement of building Norway's second Galileo station, TrollSat in Antarctica. The Norwegian Prime Minister Jens Stoltenberg holds a short speech at the laying of the

[193] http://www.ksat.no/News/Galileo-betjening.php

156

foundation stone; the content of which is not about Norway's militarization of the Polar Regions and space:

> Galileo is one of Europe's most important space projects. Among other things we will utilize it to produce reliable and functional satellite-based navigation systems. The satellite station in the south is a part of the government's northern region investment. It will provide better navigation in the northern regions.[194]

Accordingly there are many versions of what Galileo will be used for. The same applies to the other major EU satellite project, Global Monitoring for Environment and Security.

Originally the programme had another name, which was Global Monitoring for Environmental Security. Establishment of the programme was proposed by the European Commission ESA, the French space exploration organization and other organizations at a meeting in the Italian town of Baveno 19th May 1998. The aim was to develop and improve environmental monitoring in order to meet the environmental threats that were thoroughly documented during the Kyoto negotiations the previous year. It took just a year before the name was changed to Global Monitoring for Environment and Security, GMES.

In the statutes of the European Space Exploration Organisation ESA, Article two states that ESA shall engage exclusively in peaceful activity, but this does not prevent the ESA in being the EU's most important instrument in realizing GMES' and other militaries' ambitions for outer space. The powers that be resort to complex and intricate legal contortions to match the ground with the map. As Stefania Barbieri, a top ESA executive, says at the annual conference for the EU's defense organization EDU at Brussels in 2010:

---

[194] http://www.regjeringen.no/nb/dep/smk/Pressesenter/pressemeldinger/2008/--En-milepal-i-miljoovervakning-fra-sate.html?id=497487

The ESA Convention does not say that ESA is a civil agency. The Convention provides that activities must be for "peaceful purposes" interpreted in the light of international space law as "non-aggressive." The only making ESA de facto civil is the source of funding, today almost entirely civil; military funding not excluded; technologies may serve dual purposes.[195]

In that GMES want military and civilian tasks in one and the same system, it is easy to give emphasis to one rather than the other, when it suits the purpose. Naturally those developing different types of military intelligence functions in GMES are not keen on this being open to the public domain because it provides sensitive information to hostile interests that can be politically sensitive. Therefore the official information is mostly about environmental monitoring.

The little that is written about military activity is packaged in a language and form that gives the reader the impression the whole business is quite without risk and certainly above criticism. The word "military" is almost absent. This has been replaced throughout with the far more positive-toned word "security". Examples of use of the new technology are military operations that have general public support, such as combating piracy on the open seas. However, searching GMES sub-programs reveals a fair amount of public information:

> The overriding ambition of the EU and ESA is to within the space of a few years turn GMES into a unique, global, ground observation system, or if you prefer - spy satellite system – by gathering, coordinating and processing information from a number of existing European ground observation satellite systems, other non-European satellite systems and new, own satellites.

LIMES (Land and Sea Integrated Monitoring for European Security) is part of the job of filling the security aspect of GMES

---

[195] http://www.slidefinder.net/P/presentation_space_and_security_sd/1464961

with content. Ten or so companies and organizations from various European countries participate, including the Norwegian Armed Forces' Research Institute and Kongsberg Satellite Services. The task is to use satellite observation together with satellite navigation and satellite communication to develop "security programs" that includes monitoring of sea areas and so-called "critical society" structures".[196]

This means coordinating the use of satellites such as British TopSat, German Rapid Eye and TerraSar-X and Italian COSMO-SkyMed with new satellites and satellite systems that are under development. Rapid Eye, TerraSar-X and COSMO-SkyMed have, as we know, permission to use Svalsat. Thought is also given to using intelligence information from unnamed vessels, radar installations ashore and pilotless aircraft.[197]

The project has a budget of 21 million euro or around NOK 140 million, which is covered by the EU's research and development programme, again partially financed by Norway.

G-MOSAIC (GMES Services for Management of Operations, Situational Awareness and Intelligence for Regional Crises) is another development scheme with about the same size budget and same financing. The objective here is even more distinctively military: to improve intelligence efforts in crisis situations, as an aid to shaping security policy etcetera. The Italian company Telespazio heads the work. At the same time several of the major companies specializing in space exploration activities also participate. These include the French-dominated EADS Astrium, Thales and Eurosense. Add to this various countries' space exploration organizations, such as German DLR.[198]

---

[196] http://ec.europa.eu/enterprise/policies/space/files/research/limes_en.pdf
[197] http://www.fp6-limes.eu/uploads/docs/LIMES-D1000.6-TPZ-2.0.pdf

[198] http://www.gmes.info/pages-principales/projects/g-mosaic/more-on-g-mosaic/

On 7th March 2011 e-GEOS, which is an Italian sales company (owned 50 percent by the Italian State) for satellite data and satellite images issues a press release. e-GEOS has, as a coordinating company for G-MOSAIC, sold fresh images of developments in the war in Libya to the Italian armed forces. The images are of Benghazi, Tripoli and other towns where fighting is in progress. Traced on the images are gunfire, airports, roads, transport systems, embassies and medical centers. The images have been taken by Landsat, which downloads to Svalbard, and Geoeye-1, which triggered the establishment of KSAT's ground station in Antarctica.[199]

KSAT has, together with its European cooperating companies, concentrated its efforts on becoming the principal service partner for GMES, according to the company's annual report for 2005. KSAT entered into collaboration on oil production surveillance as early as in 2005. Two years later the company maintains it is one of the most important companies providing services to GMES, and is confident that both Svalsat and TrollSat will become key ground stations for the secure and rapid access to raw data from GMES-satellites.

Svalsat and TrollSat are now the key ground stations for GMES. In 2011 all satellites in GMES, Envisat, Radarsat-2, TerraSar-X, Tandem-X and COSMO-SkyMed 1–4 utilize Svalsat. Envisat and Radarsat-2 also utilize TrollSat. The Norwegian authorities are aware that the planned GMES satellites Sentinel-1, Sentinel-2 and Sentinel-3 will use TrollSat.

Back to the meeting in Parliament's European Committee in January 2010. The Minister of Trade and Commerce Trond Giske says there is not enough attention given to Norway's space exploration activities.

"It's not often we read in the newspaper about the 'space' nation Norway, but that is in fact what we are. We have an

---

[199] http://www.e-geos.it/news/11-03-09-libya/index.html

abundance of technology, competent manpower and productive companies within this area," said Giske.

My question is whether all sides of this activity are equally desirable. Further, whether the Minister of Trade and Commerce, as the cabinet minister responsible for these matters in the government, should have presented a rather broader perspective than just trade policy and political overtures to the EU at the meeting in Parliament. Trond Giske declines a request to be interviewed on Galileo and GMES.

Chapter 12
Taking the battle into space

One of China's meteorological satellites, FY-1C, has at the close of 2006 – New Year 2007 orbited round the South and North Poles for almost eight years, and is ready for replacement. In addition to traditional weather forecasts the satellite has also provided valuable information on floods and forest fires, and is used in climate research.

The advanced instruments are housed in a one-meter square, white canister. Two oblong blue solar panels on both sides of the main body provide the satellite with the power it needs. The satellite measures ten meters between the tips of the two solar panels. The satellite orbits at the same altitude as U.S. commercial and military intelligence satellites. A little over six o'clock in the morning Friday 11th January, the satellite is nearing the inner tracts of China.

Meanwhile on the ground Chinese specialists are getting ready to carry out an advanced military experiment. At the Xichang missile launch field the countdown has begun for the medium range missile HQ-19 – in the nose of which is a bullet-shaped weapon, an exoatmospheric kinetic kill vehicle, KKV. Its kinetic force will destroy the assault target on impact. The weapon has its own data-based communications and navigation systems to find and decide targets, and similar types were used with success in tests in the development of the American intercontinental nuclear missile defense shield.

The missile HQ-19 – probably a missile developed from a Russian S-400 missile or even quite simply a stolen S-400 missile – is launched at 06:28. Outside the familiar orbit for meteorology satellites the assault weapon is programmed on a course directly towards the satellite, and hits it at a speed of eight kilometers per second or 27 000 kilometers per hour. The satellite is shattered into a million splinters. This all takes place 854 kilometers above the earth's surface.[200]

It is only several days later that the episode becomes common knowledge. The successful targeting and destruction gives political leaders in a number of countries quite a jolt. Several decades have passed since the United States - during the Cold War – was the last nation to carry out experiments with the shooting down of satellites. The United States stated goal is full military control throughout space, and reacts in no uncertain terms:

"The U.S. believes China's development and testing of such weapons is inconsistent with the spirit of cooperation that both countries aspire in the civil area (…) We and other countries have expressed our concern regarding this action to the Chinese," says Gordon Johndroe, spokesman for the U.S. National Security Council.[201]

A year later the world is witness yet again to the destruction of an orbiting satellite. This time it is the United States that carries out an operation costing US$ 100 million.

On 20th February 2008 two U.S. naval vessels the USS Lake Erie and the USS Decatur are awaiting orders somewhere in the Pacific Ocean. The navy vessel the USS Russell is tied up at a quay in Pearl Harbour, Hawaii, where it will coordinate the exercise. The USS Lake Erie's primary task is to be a test vessel for the U.S. missile defense.

---

[200] see
http://www.geospatialworld.net/index.php?option=com_content&view=article&id=14238%3Afy-1c-polar-orbiting-meteorological-satellite-of-china-satellite-ground-system-and-preliminary-applications&catid=87%3Atechnology-remote-sensing&Itemid=50&limitstart=1,
http://cdi.org/program/document.cfm?DocumentID=3801&StartRow=11&ListRows=10&&Orderby=D.DateLastUpdated&ProgramID=65&typeID=(4,5)&from_page=relateditems.cfm and http://www.wired.com/dangerroom/2008/01/inside-the-chin/

[201] http://www.globalsecurity.org/space/world/china/asat.htm

On the same date Defense Secretary Robert M. Gates makes his final preparations before issuing the order. In the morning he consults with the White House, at 1 pm he gives the order to fire at one of the United States' own military intelligence satellites.

The USS Lake Erie has a crew of just less than 400 persons. It's a hectic time for representatives from arms manufacturers Lockheed Martin and Raytheon, and has been for more than a month. During the previous few days the vessel's advance instruments and other equipment have directly and indirectly kept a close eye on the satellite around the clock during its polar orbits. As with the Chinese test the Americans will also attempt to destroy a satellite through the use of kinetic energy – that is, without an explosive charge.

It's still 20th February at 10:16pm, U.S. East Coast time, and the USS Lake Erie launches a Standard Missile-3 towards the U.S. intelligence satellite USA-193. After the collision radar images on board the USS Lake Erie are totally indecipherable. Aircraft and radar installations ashore report that USA-193 has become a cloud of larger and smaller metal fragments. During the next three-four hours fiery objects from what was USA-193 rain down into the sea around the USS Lake Erie, where on board the mood is one of celebration on having accomplished a successful mission.[202]

Now it is Russia, China and other countries that react against the United States. An official statement from the Russian foreign affairs says: "Such tests mean in essence the creation of a new strategic weapon".[203] Later it becomes apparent that Russia

---

202

http://www.spacelaw.olemiss.edu/publications/USA193%20Selected%20Documents.pdf

[203] http://www.defensenews.com/story.php?i=3378279

and India are also developing and have the technology to destroy satellites.[204]

China protests: "We demand that the US... swiftly brief the international community with necessary data and information in time, so that relevant countries can take preventative measures".

The United States rejects the criticism, and the Pentagon claims the intelligence satellite which had the toxic substance hydrazine on board was out of control, and it was therefore necessary to destroy it before it fell to earth and injured people. It was not a test of a new arms system.

Researchers in several countries voiced strong doubts about this explanation. Firstly, it was claimed that the toxic matter would almost certainly have incinerated on its passage through the atmosphere, secondly it was highly unlikely the satellite would have hit a populated area.[205]

The Secure World Foundation is a renowned American foundation headed by Ray Williamson, which for many years has served in an expert advisory capacity for the U.S. Congress. An announcement issued by the foundation states the United States is sending an entirely wrong message to the global community. The foundation maintains that few will see any significant difference between the United States using a missile to destroy a clandestine U.S. satellite and the Chinese shooting down a weather satellite 850 kilometers above the earth's surface.

But therein does NOT lie an end to the conflict between the United States and China. 11th January 2010 China launches a CSS-X-11 missile from the Korla base and destroys a Chinese long-

---

[204] See http://www.commondreams.org/view/2009/03/20-9 and http://bx.businessweek.com/india-and-china-science/view?url=http%3A%2F%2Ffeedproxy.google.com%2F~r%2Fyankeesailor%2Fngse%2F~3%2FWdChS7gaJys%2Findia-is-fast-pacing-development-of-its.html
[205] http://www.commondreams.org/archive/2008/04/02/8048

range missile in its orbit. American intelligence is convinced this is a new test an anti-satellite weapon.[206]

Two days later the Obama administration sends an official protest to China, and reiterates that the same level of anxiety still exists regarding Chinese policy that prevailed during President Bush' term of office. Exactly one month later an airborne American military aircraft successfully carries out a test shooting down of a long-range missile using a laser.[207]

Released WikiLeaks documents provide more information. The United States was far more critical to China's first test than the reaction published in the public domain. The U.S. Secretary of State Condoleezza Rice threatened China by answering with "military" countermeasures to protect American satellites. Nonetheless the USA meant that diplomacy wasn't enough. The U.S. Secretary of Defense Robert Gates decided – with support from Bush – that the United States would execute its own mission to destroy a satellite. The WikiLeaks documents confirm that the destruction of the USA-193 was a military "test", and not a necessary operation to spare the environment, as was claimed by the Pentagon.

What is the real attitude of the United States toward military activity in space?[208]

The United States has long since been planning to make space into a new arena for war. President Ronald Reagan's Star Wars plan from 1983 is well known, which in its original form was shelved after a few years. However, since Reagan's time in office the United States has worked continuously to gain full military control of space. A plan for the United States Space Command from 1998 under President Bill Clinton reveals America's ambitions in no

---

[206] http://www.telegraph.co.uk/news/worldnews/wikileaks/8299410/WikiLeaks-timeline-of-the-space-race.html
[207] See previous note
[208] http://www.telegraph.co.uk/news/worldnews/wikileaks/8299491/WikiLeaks-US-vs-China-in-battle-of-the-anti-satellite-space-weapons.html

uncertain terms. The document, "United States Space Command Vision 2020", begins with two sentences that could have been taken straight out of a science fiction film:

> US Space Command – dominating the space dimension of military operations to protect US interests and investment. Integrating Space Forces into warfighting capabilities across the full spectrum of conflict.[209]

The line of thinking is plain to see: The military's task is to protect American economic and security-political interests. Back in the days of the Wild West it was the cavalry that accompanied new settlers out to the West and secured railroads and new settlements, before the U.S. Navy eventually patrolled the seven seas as a support for American interests. Nowadays radar systems, satellites and missiles must be utilized to defend military and civilian satellites, which have become a crucial component of the U.S. community machinery. It's only to be expected that space – in likeness with sea, land and air – becomes the new arena for war.

The U.S. Space Command is now the U.S. Air Force Space Command, which has 46 000 employees and military plant/installations and personnel spread across the entire globe. The U.S. Air Force Space Command is in charge of the intercontinental nuclear missiles and a number of other arms systems that utilize space.

Since 2001 the U.S. Air Force has often carried out a particular exercise, the Schriever Wargame, which in practical terms examines how a war in space would develop in this day and age. For the first time last year (2010) the USA's closest allies – the United Kingdom, Australia and Canada also participated. In 2010 the Schriever Wargame assembled 600 intelligence personnel, higher-ranking military officials and other decision-makers. Deputizing for the U.S. President was Ambassador Lincoln P. Bloomfield, who was also personal advisor for President George W. Bush. Experiences gained from the Schriever

---

[209] http://www.fas.org/spp/military/docops/usspac/visbook.pdf

167

Wargame, which to a large extent is a war exercise played out via computers, have been decisive in regard to new purchases for the U.S. space defense.

Despite the U.S. Defense's traditional attitude of all-embracing candor, the U.S. Air Force Command is discreet about giving out information about the exercise. However, a 17-page PowerPoint presentation on the Schriever Wargame 2010 from The Space Innovation and Development Center, which is a part of the U.S. Air Force Space Command, provides a tiny pointer as to how far the United States has come in planning for war in space.[210]

Green is the enemy in the war game. A green circle is divided into four sectors. Titles of the four sectors are written inside each; ISLAMIC WORLD, EURASIA, SOUTH ASIA and OTHERS, thus denoting the sources that currently represent a threat to the United States.

Green fights blue. The blue are representatives for American military organizations together with allies. Not surprisingly these include representatives from NGA, other U.S. intelligence organizations and NASA.

How does the USA envisage such a war? A wall chart shows a ground station aiming a beam towards a satellite, beside the letters "OCS" – Offensive Counter Space. The United States has not been willing to admit publicly that the country has arms capable of attacking in space. Regardless, development of laser weapons has almost certainly advanced so much that this capacity must surely exist.

A heading titled; "SW 10 Initial Insights", Schriever Wargames 2010's first lessons learned. Here we have a reappearance of the line of thinking in the U.S. Space Command

---

[210]

www.spacewarfare.org/.../Briefings%202010/7%20Vincent%20SIDC_SW10_1 0%20Jun%2010.ppt

Vision 2020 from 1998, on achieving full military control in order to secure U.S. global, economic interests:

> Asymmetric capabilities are essential for escalation control, protection of global economic interests – and may be cheaper!

It is claimed that commercial satellites could play a major role in acting as a deterrent, but the question is whether these would be "available" during a war. It can mean that war planners believe ground stations for commercial satellites would be destroyed or in some other way be made inoperable in the event of an outbreak of war.

Lincoln P. Bloomfield, who played the American president in the exercise, wrote an article about his experiences in the U.S. Air Force Space Command's journal High Frontier in November 2010.[211] In his opinion the biggest difference between a situation where the use of nuclear arms is considered and a situation where the use of space-based weapons could be used, is that the world has no experience on which to a base a decision for the use of space-based weapons. Bloomfield says it clearly limits the options available to the president and his advisors in dealing with future crises in the situation room in The White House.

In previous crises between the United States and other nuclear arms powers the conflicts have built up over time, and it has been possible to initiate measures to avoid war and to prepare oneself for war. For instance, divisions have been put on the alert for a higher level of contingency, and negotiations are started with a counterpart. Bloomfield believes a space and data war would appear without warning and paralyses the most important satellites and data centers that control power, telecommunications and transport systems.

The previous personal advisor to President Bush stresses the importance of allied countries' satellite systems and ground

---

[211] http://www.afspc.af.mil/shared/media/document/AFD-101020-017.pdf

systems for supporting the United States as direct contributors during a crisis situation, also with technical expertise. Norway has to some extent been a world leader in monitoring of the seas, and can be a crucial contributor.

The militarization of space has already cost many lives. The Pentagon has long been eager to have satellites that use radioactive materials as a source of energy. That was the reason for NASA previously insisting on using radioactive material, even though solar cell technology was available. On 21st April 1964 the American navigation satellite SNAP-9A collapses during the launch with half kilo plutonium on board. The plutonium was of the worst sort, plutonium-238, which is 280 times more radioactive than plutonium-239, which is used in nuclear arms. The deadly material is disseminated worldwide.

Dr. John Gofman, Professor of Medicine at the world-renowned Berkeley University in California, believes the incident resulted in an upsurge in cases of lung cancer in the world.
"Even though it is impossible to calculate the increase in number of cases of lung cancer due to the accident, there is no doubt that the discharge of so much plutonium-238 has led to more diagnosed cases of lung cancer over several subsequent decades," said Gofman.[212]

An incident with the space probe Cassini in 1999 could have ended with a far graver outcome. Inside this probe was around ten times more plutonium-238 than was the case with the accident in 1964. The probe was guided from ground control towards the gravitation field in order for it to gain speed to take it into orbit. Fortunately the probe's descent was halted before it entered the gravitation field. If it hadn't, the probe would have incinerated and showered the earth with plutonium-238. The probe was not fitted with heat shields.[213]

---

[212] Karl Grossman, *Weapons in Space*, The Open Media Pamphlet Series
[213] See previous note

23rd September the same autumn NASA's March Climate Orbiter came too close to Mars and crashed on the planet. This could have easily happened with Cassini. The cause of the accident was that the company Lockheed Martin and NASA's Jet Propulsion Laboratory used feet and meters respectively in their work with the project.[214]

Gofman estimates that 950 000 people would have died if Cassini had entered the earth's atmosphere. Dr. Ernest Sternglass, Professor in radiological physics at the University of Pittsburgh, estimates the number fatalities would have been between 20 and 40 million.[215]

The book *Military Space Forces: The Next 50 Years* from 1989 presents a frightening picture of American military ambitions in space. A congress dominated by the usually more moderate democrats had ordered the book. The Congress was eager that it "should be a reference work for [...] military space policy, programme and budget".[216]

The author, John M. Collins, researcher at the American Congress' library, proposes military bases on the moon to defend U.S. mining plant there, and to also protect the transport passage between the moon and the earth. The author even maintains that U.S. forces shall be used to deprive other countries of the possibility to transport of minerals from the moon to the earth.

Furthermore Collins claims that use of nuclear power is essential to secure enough energy for military forces in space. On the book's back cover Leo Aspin, a Democrat from Wisconsin is quoted; "No other military space study puts all pieces of the puzzle together. Professionals and the public both should find it valuable".

---

[214] See note 212
[215] See note 212
[216] John M. Collins, *Military Space Forces: The Next 50 Years*

171

Aspin later becomes the Secretary of Defense for Bill Clinton.

Many had faith that there would be a real change in American policy with Barack Obama as the new president, also in regard to space security policy. The tactics used in the election campaign were new. Obama said he feared China's successful test of the anti-satellite weapon in 2007 was the beginning of a new arms race in space, but he would not meet this situation with new American arms. In the election campaign Barack Obama was opposed to development of anti-satellite weaponry and arms in space. He meant the USA had to "demonstrate strong leadership by including other nations in discussions on how one could prevent the slow trend towards turning space into a new war arena".[217]

This was a completely different tune from that of the sitting president, George W. Bush. He meant the USA "had to respond to interference, and also deny, if necessary, opponents use of their space capabilities that are hostile to American national interests." His policy was to oppose all proposals on international restrictions of arms in space.

Naturally the major American arms manufacturers were on tenterhooks. For many years development of space technology for the Pentagon had been their support beam. A new course would have drastic consequences.

Seconds after Obama took the oath as a new American president on 20th January 2009, The White House website was updated with the new president's views on a number of political issues. There you would have read that Obama was eager for "a global ban on weapons that can damage military and civilian satellites".[218] This text was later removed from The White House's website.

---

[217] http://www.reuters.com/article/2009/01/25/us-usa-obama-space-idUSTRE50O15X20090125
[218]
http://www.cdi.org/program/issue/document.cfm?DocumentID=4486&IssueID=

The text now on the website, is completely in keeping with what has been U.S. policy for several decades:

> "The full spectrum of U.S. military capabilities depends on our space systems. To maintain our technological edge and protect assets in this domain, we will continue to invest in next-generation capabilities such as operationally responsive space and global positioning systems. We will cooperate with our allies and the private sector to identify and protect against intentional and unintentional threats to U.S. and allied space capabilities".

On 28th June 2010 the White House Press Office announces Barack Obama's guidelines for a new national space policy, which will supersede a corresponding plan George W. Bush had from 2006. Neither here was there a single word about a ban against arms in space or anxiety about a new arms race. Instead it was emphasized that:"[219] The United States will employ a variety of measures to help assure the use of space for all responsible parties, and, consistent with the inherent right of self-defense, deter others from interference and attack, defend our space systems and contribute to the defense of allied space systems, and, if deterrence fails, defeat efforts to attack them".

Yet again it is apparent that there isn't necessarily any difference between a Republican and a Democrat as the President in The White House. American arms manufacturers don't need to worry about being out of work in the immediate future. The on-going build of the U.S. missile defense is the dearest arms system yet embarked on.[220]

76&StartRow=1&ListRows=10&appendURL=&Orderby=DateLastUpdated&ProgramID=68&issueID=0

[219] http://www.globalsecurity.org/jhtml/jframe.html#http://www.globalsecurity.org/space/library/policy/national/100628_national_space_policy.pdf|||

[220] http://www.cdi.org/program/document.cfm?DocumentID=4371&from_page=../index.cfm

Since Ronald Reagan's famous Star Wars speech in 1985, more than USD 150 billion has been spent on missile defense, calculated according to figures from Congress. In 2010 under Obama, the Missile Defense Agency, which is responsible for the development and installation of the controversial nuclear missile defense system, had a budget of around NOK 50 billion.[221]

The Pentagon has requested a minimum of US$ 62.5 billion for missile defense for the next five years alone, without prospects of funding requirements declining. For instance the Pentagon with Obama's blessing has plans to build an advanced and costly shield in Europe to counter intercontinental attacks, which will be completed in the year 2020 at the earliest.

One reason for the massive amounts spent on research, development, testing and placement is that the technical challenges of building a missile defense system are enormous – greater by far than constructing a new generation of aircraft carriers, fighter aircraft or any new type of arms system. This is according to the State Secretary of the U.S. Defense Department and Director for testing of new arms systems under President Bill Clinton, Philip E. Coyle.

Successfully destroying an intercontinental nuclear missile travelling towards the United States in the course of its around 20 minutes' long journey in space has been compared with shooting a rifle bullet towards another rifle bullet that is already airborne. Coyle reckons the task is much more difficult, namely because an enemy will also simultaneously launch many harmless missiles and create other barriers and decoys, making it difficult to follow and destroy the real target.

On 25th February 2009 Coyle was invited to a hearing in the House Committee on Armed Services, a section of the U.S.

221

http://worldsecurityinstitute.org/temp/Missile%20Defense%20Budget%20Requ est%20FY10.pdf

Congress that is responsible for allocation of funds to the U.S. Department of Defense, where he said:

> To use a popular analogy, shooting down an enemy missile going 17,000 mph out in space is like trying to hit a hole-in-one in golf when the hole is going 17,000 mph. If an enemy uses decoys and countermeasures, missile defense is shooting a hole-in-one when the hole is going 17,000 mph and the green is covered with black circles the same size as the hole. The defender doesn't know which target to aim for.[222]

The Missile Defense Agency does not agree. The agency's website states categorically that radar systems and missiles already protect the United States, and it is proud of its history:

> "More than 25 years ago, President Ronald Reagan challenged the U.S. scientific community to develop antiballistic missile technologies that would improve our national security and reduce our reliance on nuclear weapons. Today, the Missile Defense Agency, or MDA, is answering that challenge."[223]

Back to the hearing in the American Congress: Philip E. Coyle, who for many years was in charge of testing the arms system at the Pentagon, concludes with comments concerning a possible situation where the missile shield would be put into use:

> The Pentagon does not explain it, but the Congress will remember that if we ever need to rely on missile defenses against enemy ICBMs it would be in an environment where nuclear weapons are exploding, even in an all-out nuclear war.
> In all-out nuclear war, some of those enemy missiles could reach their targets, including the ones that U.S. missile defenses miss. Some enemy ICBMs might be equipped with warhead fuses to go off before an approaching interceptor would reach them.

---

[222] http://www.cdi.org/pdfs/CoyleHASCfull2_25_091.pdf

[223] http://www.mda.mil/

175

Some enemy ICBMs might be deliberately triggered to explode at high altitude, to cause Electromagnetic Pulse (EMP) interference that can disrupt U.S. military command and control including U.S. missile defense command and control systems.[224]

Fort Greely is an American military base near the town of Fairbanks in Alaska. In 30-metre deep underground silos are 26 missiles in readiness 24/7, 365 days of the year to meet any threat against the United States. President George W. Bush selected the site in 2002, so that the USA could readily respond to an attack from North Korea, China, Russia, Iran and other countries in Asia and the Middle East. The last missile was placed in position as recently as the autumn of 2010 – 16 meters tall and 1.2 meters wide.

The American base is well protected due to its secluded location, double fences and stringent security guarding of the base. More than five kilometers of underground tunnels link the silos, control center and other sections of the plant. All buildings are constructed from special steel as protection against hostile attack and nuclear explosions in space. [225]

The armaments at Fort Greely and a corresponding complex at Vandenberg Air Force Base in California are now the most important weapons in the American intercontinental missile defense, described by Obama as "proven and effective". But in order for the missiles to function, it is absolutely essential to have knowledge about the hostile missile attack, both before and during the launch. A global network of radar systems and satellites shall enable this.

New satellites shall detect intercontinental missile launches with the aid of infrared sensors that register heat generated during the missile launch. Two satellites will have fixed positions above the equator, while two satellites will orbit the earth. The SBIRS-

---

[224] See note 221

[225] http://www.newsminer.com/view/full_story/6563679/article-New-missile-installed-at-Fort-Greely?instance=home_news_window_left_top_2 and http://www.missilethreat.com/missiledefensesystems/id.18/system_detail.asp

High satellite system has encountered major technical problems, is several years behind schedule and is still not fully operative. The budget has been overspent by many billions of dollars.[226]

For the time being the missile defense system must make do with the Defense Support Program satellites. It is an alarm system that has been in existence for more than 30 years, but was kept secret for many years. The new SBIRS-High satellite system will be able to detect a launch twice as fast and provide much more information than the old system.

Planners of the American star wars also intend to have separate satellites that on the basis of information about the launch will track and tail the hostile missile in its orbit over the atmosphere. Originally the plan was to have 24 such STSS satellites. At the start of 2011 the status was such that two experimental satellites had been in space for a year. It will still take a long time and require huge sums of money before satellites in space can track and tail missiles.[227]

Nonetheless, those who sit with their fingers on the launch button of the intercontinental anti-missiles at Fort Greely in Alaska and at Vandenberg Air Force Base in California, have many more tools they can utilize in tracking a hostile attack. At present 21 large and small American warships track an intercontinental missile as it orbits outside the atmosphere – in 2013 31 warships will have this capacity. The radar component of the Aegis arms system on these ships, produced by Lockheed Martin, has proved in tests to be effective in following medium-range and long-range missiles.[228]

The missile defense is also supported by American radar systems located across the globe. It stretches from the Aleutians

---

[226] http://www.afspc.af.mil/library/factsheets/factsheet.asp?id=3675

[227] http://www.mda.mil/news/11news0004.html

[228] http://www.strategypage.com/htmw/htada/articles/20110422.aspx

west of Alaska in the Pacific Ocean, via Vardø, Fylingdales in the United Kingdom, Thule on Greenland and to Beale in California. A drilling rig, designed and built in Russia by the Reitan group, Vital Forsikring and other Norwegian interests, now functions as a floating radar system for missile defense. The rig can be positioned in any ocean or sea, as required.[229] In December 2010 it was anchored in the harbor in Hawaii. The cost for this radar system alone is over one billion dollars. The United States now has six other transportable radar systems for missile defense, two of which are now positioned in Japan and Israel respectively.

An ingenious system for communication and control has been built amongst all the components of the missile system. Fiber cables and satellite communications are a vital part of this. There is also comprehensive research and development work being carried out on other weapons and weapon systems.

One of the most controversial is designed to attack hostile missiles from space, either with laser or kinetic energy. For many years the Missile Defense Agency has had a project called "The Missile Defense Test Bed". The objective has been to position satellites with offensive weapons in space, with all relevant equipment for communications and command systems.[230]

The organization of research scientists – The Union of Concerned Scientists is highly critical, of whether the system will be able to function due to the enormous costs. Nonetheless it is pointed out that such a system could be effective in attacking satellites, which are easier to target and which move slower than an intercontinental missile. The Union of Concerned Scientists fears that other countries would thereby feel forced to develop a similar weapon.[231]

---

[229] http://www.bt.no/nyheter/innenriks/Her-er-Norges-bidrag-til-USAs-rakettforsvar-1844066.html

[230] see
http://www.ucsusa.org/nuclear_weapons_and_global_security/space_weapons/policy_issues/the-missile-defense-space.html and
http://www.cdi.org/pdfs/SpaceWeaponsFY09.pdf

178

How far then has progress been made with arms systems whose primary task is to attack satellites? And how far have they come in being able to defend own satellites?

There is technology in the world today designed to directly attack or disrupt a satellite in four different ways.[232] (Damage can also be inflicted on a satellite system by destruction of ground installations and communications.) The most well-known method of attacking a satellite is to launch a missile from earth as did the United States in 2008, China in 2007 and the Soviet Union for the last time in 1982.

A much less known method is satellites that are put into orbit and that can "sleep" for many years before becoming active by positioning itself as close as possible to a hostile satellite. From there the satellite can either commence a direct attack, disrupt the other satellite's communications with earth or physically block the other satellite's possibilities to take images of the earth.

The fact is that Russia had these satellites deployed as a part of its military contingency up until 1991. Indications are that China and the United States now also have this type of satellite. The Pentagon has run development projects for small, highly maneuverable satellites for a number of years and has also employed clandestine satellites to investigate a warning missile that no longer functioned for the missile defense system.

China launched its manned space shuttle Shenzhou-7 in September 2008, followed by a satellite in the same orbit the day after. The satellite that followed behind moved around the manned space shuttle and took photos that were later communicated to earth. Thus China had also demonstrated that they master the technique needed to use satellites to destroy, disrupt and spy on other satellites.

---

[231] See previous note
[232] https://www.afresearch.org/skins/.../display.aspx?rs...

The third way to attack a satellite is to use a laser or powerful microwaves, which can be launched from the ground, air or space. As early as in the eighties the Soviet Union had developed laser weapons with a long enough range to be used from the ground against satellites.

According to Donald Kerr, the former Director of the American National Reconnaissance Office, NRO, China has in at least one instance blinded an American intelligence satellite with the use of lasers.[233] For its part the United States is by no means trailing behind. MIRACLE, which is a ground-based infrared chemical laser, was developed for two tasks: One to contribute toward developing defense and countermeasures against hostile laser attacks, the other to be a weapon against hostile satellites.[234]

The fourth method for destroying satellites in orbit is to employ a nuclear weapon. A nuclear explosion will create electromagnetic waves that destroy all electronics in the proximity. "Starfish Prime" was an American experiment conducted in 1964 that showed just how destructive a nuclear explosion can be. A 1.4-megaton bomb was detonated at an altitude of 400 kilometers over the Pacific Ocean. The explosion resulted in extensive damage to many of the satellites orbiting closest to the earth, but also damaged American and British satellites 600 kilometers higher up in space.

For a nation that has just begun consolidating space capacity or that does not have space capacity, such a weapon represents a unique opportunity to fight against the otherwise so dominant United States. As the USA's dependency on satellites is common knowledge, each and every nation with a certain amount of knowledge of missile technology and access to nuclear arms could carry out such an attack and destroy satellites in orbit as well

---

[233] http://www.spacenews.com/archive/archive06/chinalaser_1002.html

[234] http://www.rand.org/pubs/monograph_reports/2005/MR1649.pdf

as preventing satellites from utilizing some areas of space for a considerable length of time.

These evaluations are not made by Al-Qaida or some hostile state, but extracted from a report produced by the U.S. Air Defense's own university in Alabama and authored by Major Jason C. Eisenreich.[235] He points out that countries such as Russia, China, India, Pakistan, Iran and North Korea can carry out this type of explosion, and are naturally also aware that such an operation would adversely affect their own country's satellites.

Is there no international co-operation to stop this militarization? Are there no agreements that can stop this trend?

Ever since the world's first satellite Sputnik was launched into space in 1957, there have been powerful forces to avoid militarization and warfare in space. The President of the United States from 1953 to 1961, Dwight D. Eisenhower, saw the dangers, and the former general maintained it was essential for the international community to unite on utilizing "space for peaceful purposes". It was the international agreement on peaceful utilisation of Antarctica, built on successful international research cooperation, which was the guideline for the "Space Treaty" of 1967.[236]

The "Space Treaty" states that the moon and all other planets in space do not belong to any single country, and are only permitted used for peaceful purposes. A nation can plant a flag, as the United States did on the moon in 1969, but not claim sovereignty. No military installations of any sort are permitted; no testing of arms, no military exercises. Military personnel are welcome, but only in connection with civilian research activity and other "peaceful activity". The formulation on military activity is the same as in the Antarctic Treaty.

---

[235] See note 232
[236] http://www.armscontrol.org/documents/outerspace

The space between the moon and earth falls to a large extent outside the treaty. The treaty text prohibits nuclear arms and other mass destruction arms, but is vague in regard to other military use. When the treaty was entered into, the Cold War had already given the United States and the Soviet Union spy, communication and early warning satellites, and satellites were regarded as too valuable to warrant prohibition. Besides no one could have foreseen the colossal technical development that would inevitably cause satellites to become - in the space of just 20 years – an integral part of any war-like activities. Such a development would have only been described in a science fiction novel.

At the close of the seventies there were many countries that realized there were too many gaps in the treaty, which were being exploited by the United States and the Soviet Union. Ever since 1981 a particular resolution, Prevention of an Arms Race in Space, PAROS, has regularly been raised on the United Nation's (UN) agenda. Both China and Russia supported the resolution. China has also presented proposals of their own, supported by Russia. China has warned: Without a new agreement other countries will be forced to attempt to catch up to the United States' USA's military lead.[237] The USA has effectively blocked this effort because the resolution on security policy in the UN General Assembly must be approved unanimously. 2nd December 2008 the matter was for example raised in the United Nations (UN) General Assembly. 177 voted for, the United States was the only country to vote against. This came as no surprise. Everyone in the assembly already knew what the outcome would be.[238]

237

http://www.un.org/disarmament/HomePage/ODAPublications/ODAUpdate/2008/March/index.html

[238] http://www.un.org/News/Press/docs/2008/ga10792.doc.htm

Chapter 13
Radar for the European missile shield

It's still January in Finnmark and winter is at its harshest. It's dark when I get up, and still dark when I start to drive the two hours it takes to get from Vadsø on the north side of the Varangerfjord to Kirkenes on the south side of the fjord. Many long, desolate stretches. Not much to fix one's eyes on. Despite snowdrifts threatening to block the road, I'm focused on keeping my speed up. Kirkenes has a direct flight to Oslo.

At Kirkenes airport by chance I bump into Rolf Einar Mortensen, the chairman of Vardø Borough Council, the borough that has the world's most advanced radar, Globus II.[239] We start talking about the radar. He thinks the municipality, suffering under the effects of negative migration, should have received a tad more in the municipal coffers for its military installations.

"I once saw an overview of what the American radar we have on Vårberget was worth. My word, it certainly wasn't peanuts. On top of which they (the Americans) are exempt from paying property tax because the State regulations provides exceptions for defense installations. I think that's wrong. I think it's only fair that we as a municipality should get a better return on this." says Mortensen.

Vardø's Council Chairman possibly has a point there. In the course of a few decades the population of Vardø has been halved, a development that has been actively stimulated from the Norwegian State's side by the elimination of 200 State jobs. In the same period Vardø has gained an ever-increasing number of advanced military installations, with huge significance for both Norway and Norway's most important ally, the United States.

---

[239] E-mail from Captain Angie Blair, Press Division U.S. Air Force Command

I tell him I am on my way to San Francisco and Montreal to get information about the latest military development in Vardø, the Globus II radar. That's all I say, he doesn't ask any questions. Mortensen naturally also knows about the discussion concerning the radar's role for the controversial American missile defense system. Nonetheless I get the feeling he thinks it a little strange I am travelling halfway round the world to find out more about the Vardø radar.

On 25th March 1998 is the first time the general public gets to hear about Globus II. Towards the back of the daily Aftenposten this day is a small article with the following heading: "Super-radar to monitor debris in outer space". The article is based on a press release from the Norwegian High Command the previous day.[240] Journalist Inge Sellevåg of the newspaper Bergens Tidende reads the article and is immediately skeptical about charting of space debris being the real reason for placing a new military super-radar on the border to Russia. The Bergen journalist, with several exposures of the (Norwegian) Armed Forces behind him, starts searching the Internet for other explanations.

It turns out Globus II is a name the Norwegian military intelligence service has given an American radar that is actually called Have Stare, or AN/FPS-129. Originally it was the U.S. intelligence service that had the principal responsibility for the radar. Later it was used in tests for development of the controversial intercontinental nuclear missile defense system at Vandenberg Air Force Base in California. It was moved to Vardø sometime after this.

The nuclear missile defense system is designed to be used against aggressive nuclear attacks, but it also provides the United States with the capability to initiate a nuclear first strike with less risk of suffering a counterattack. This gives the United States military superiority in relation to other nuclear powers, which in

---

[240] http://www.fas.org/spp/military/program/track/980324-globus2.htm

turn will try to catch up or surpass the United States – and a new arms race is a reality.[241]

The issue of the Vardø radar takes on political overtones at the highest level. Both the United States and Russia have signed the ABM agreement that prohibits both countries from building an intercontinental missile defense system. Russia suspects the new radar in Vardø of being a part of a U.S. missile defense system, and voices heavy criticism against the United States and Norway.

In a press release issued on 25th February 2000 the Norwegian Minister of Defense Eldbjørg Løwer admitted that the radar called Globus II is the American radar Have Stare. Nonetheless she denies the radar has any connection whatsoever with an American missile defense system. The radar has had its technical specifications changed, and is therefore unsuitable for missile defense, was the explanation given.[242]

The matter sparks as much interest in other countries as it does in Norway. The British newspaper The Guardian sends its own people to Vardø. Just before the visit a storm had blown away the cover that hides and protects the actual radar. The reporter from The Guardian notices that the radar is pointing east towards Russia. He thinks the story of this radar being used to monitor space debris does not tally at all.

Even though Bergens Tidende constantly publishes new information, for some unknown reason none of the major Oslo editorial writers follow up. I team up with Inge Sellevåg at Bergens Tidende, and receive new articles from him a day in advance, so that as an NRK journalist in Vadsø I can prepare separate versions for NRK Finnmark, which enables Bergens Tidende to gain wider

---

[241] http://www.fas.org/spp/military/program/track/980324-globus2.htm

[242] http://www.regjeringen.no/nb/dokumentarkiv/Regjeringen-Bondevik-I/fd/Nyheter-og-pressemeldinger/2000/globus_ii-radaren_og_norsk_overvakning.html?id=242452

coverage for their articles. One article in particular sparks my interest more and more.

It emerges that American experts – with backgrounds from the Pentagon and American intelligence – are just shaking their heads in disbelief at what Løwer and others in the Norwegian Armed Forces are saying about the new American radar in Vardø. Professor Theodore Postol of the Massachusetts Institute of Technology, one of the foremost radar experts in the world, says there's not a shadow of doubt that the Vardø radar will provide data that enables missiles in California and Alaska to attack nuclear missiles launched from Russia.[243]

SV's defense-policy spokesman Hallgeir Langeland raises the matter in Parliament many times, but the party is left standing alone with its criticism. The Labour Party's Minister of Defense Bjørn Tore Godal mocks Langeland from the parliamentary rostrum on the significance of the Bergens Tidende's articles, saying: "To the extent one reads Bergens Tidende outside Norway and hears the representative Langeland ask questions in Parliament, you might get the impression there are many that believe there is something in this".[244]

The same year Inge Sellevåg and Bergens Tidende receive the Norwegian Press' highest distinction, '*Den store journalistprisen*', (equivalent of 'Journalist of the Year Award') for precisely the articles on the American radar in Finnmark County.

June 2002, and the U.S. President George W. Bush pulls the USA out of the ABM agreement, and grants a sum in the billions to the controversial arms system. The Russian authorities continue to bring up the Vardø radar in meetings with the Norwegian authorities, but the matter eventually dies out.

---

[243] http://www.commondreams.org/views/030200-106.htm

[244] Ordinary Question Time 24th May 2000, Norwegian Parliamentary Minutes

187

I continue to use the Internet to find out more about the Vardø radar. By combining search words such as the American term for the radar Have Stare, with the type of radar, which is X-band, and "missile defense", there emerges a glut of information – totally different from the information issued from the Norwegian intelligence service. A document that Inge Sellevåg also discovered, I found particularly interesting. It is a description of the radar and its tasks prepared by Raytheon, the company that built the radar and which was in charge of moving it from the United States to Norway:

> "Its current primary mission is to collect data on deep-space satellites, and its secondary missions are near-earth satellite tracking and data collection on missile and aerodynamic targets." [245]

It's the phrase "gather data on missiles and aerodynamic targets" that captures my interest. Vardø is the ideal location in terms of tracking intercontinental missiles from Plesetsk in Archangel to Kamtsjatka, six time zones further east. Information on orbits for Russian intercontinental missiles and arms systems are of enormous significance in enabling the USA to shoot down a nuclear weapon.

I e-mail Raytheon and receive confirmation that the information on the website was correct at the time the website was established. The website was last updated 23rd September 1999 – which is after the radar was moved from California to Vardø.

It strikes me it would be fascinating to make a TV programme about the Vardø radar, and the Vardø radar is given the thumbs up as the theme for an NRK Brennpunkt production. Several of the internationally recognized experts that Bergens Tidende had used in its reportages, reconfirm Vardø radar's usefulness for the American missile shield, as with John E. Pike, head of GlobalSecurity.org in Washington:

---

[245] http://www.armscontrol.ru/start/docs/HaveStareRaytheonWebPage.pdf

"There are in any case three ties between the radar and the missile defense. The most obvious is that it gathers information about Russian test launches. The second is that due to the radar's northern position it is openly exposed to Aurora Borealis, which can be used to examine the effects of nuclear explosions for radar installations. The third tie is due to the radar's geographic location – it is ideally positioned to rapidly provide data in the event of a missile attack on the United States," he said.

Pike has participated in hearings in the American Congress on numerous occasions, and is often engaged as an expert for CNN, BBC, ABC and other TV channels.

Meanwhile both the producer Pål Sommer-Erichson and are aware that skepticism towards Bergens Tidendes' revelations is widespread in many circles; we must have even better sources to be taken seriously. The best way is to hear it from the U.S. military apparatus itself. This should provide the necessary credibility.

One day early in June 2005 I'm having lunch with Sommer-Erichson and photographer Øystein Hillestad at a small restaurant on the outskirts of Washington's center. The telephone rings; it's Philip E. Coyle on the line. Coyle was an Under-Secretary of Defense from 1994 to 2001, with responsibility for all testing of new arms systems. Now he sits on a commission appointed by President George W. Bush to close down military bases. He is very busy with meetings on Capitol Hill, but has a little time to spare for an interview if we meet him immediately at the hotel. We hurry to pay for our lunch and jog up to the hotel where we rig up in all haste ready for an in interview in a hotel room.

Coyle arrives. He turns out to be a tall, older man with white hair and a beard, a firm handshake and direct, but friendly glance. He stresses again that he has very little time. Without much pre-chat Coyle sits in the chair we've set out for him. I ask why the radar has been moved from the United States to Norway.

"Norway is important because it's near Russia and very near China. And because the shortest distance if missiles are

189

launched towards the USA (USA's east coast, author's remark) from Russia or China is over the North Pole. Therefore a radar in Norway is important, not just because it is near Russia and China, but also because it is on the way to the United States."

"So it's very important for the missile defense?"
"Yes."

Key Norwegian politicians refuse to appear in the programme. The Minister of Defense (from the Conservative Party), Kristin Krohn Devold, says no. The chairperson of Parliament's Defense Committee, Marit Nybakk (Labour Party), backs out from an interview appointment with no explanation given after I have travelled specially from Finnmark far north in Norway to Oslo just to interview her.

The Chairman of the Parliamentary Foreign Affairs Committee, Thorbjørn Jagland, wants all the questions sent to him in advance before he will say yes or no to an interview. This is not the norm in the Norwegian press to send questions beforehand, and no interview is conducted with him either. 11th October 2005 the documentary on the Vardø radar, which I call "Pentagons Øye" ("The Eye of the Pentagon") is aired on Norwegian television.
    I really have no idea what to expect of political reactions, but I'm surprised that it is quiet, silent in fact.

This is two days after autumn's winners of the parliamentary election, the Labour Party (AP), the Centre Party (SP) and Socialist-Left Party (SV), have reached agreement on a political platform for the new coalition government, the Soria Moria Declaration. It is SV's first time in the government. SV has no objection to a formulation in the Soria Moria Declaration stating the new government says a definite no to the American missile shield:

> The Government's aim is that Norway shall work towards shelving the current plans for missile defense, and take the initiative to increase focus on early warning and prevention of conflicts.[246]

Immediately after the new government is in place, it is decided the cabinet secretary for the Ministry of Foreign Affairs, Kjetil Skogrand, and the cabinet secretary for the Ministry of Defense, Espen Barth Eide, will contact the Intelligence service to investigate whether the Vardø radar is used by the American missile defense. The conclusion after contact is that the Vardø radar does not communicate with U.S. Air Force Space Command in "real-time", and therefore the Vardø radar does not contribute to the American missile defense system.[247]

There can be cause to query the politicians' investigations into the matter. "Real-time" communication nowadays is everything from answering a phone call to e-mail and other type of electronic communication, which is a customary part of all modern cooperation. Brian Weeden, who until 2008 worked with space analyses at the 21st Space Wing of U.S. Air Force Space Command, and who we will meet later in chapter 14, also said then they received the information they wanted just by making a phone call to Vardø without any further formalities.

Additionally, which also becomes quite apparent in the programme, the Vardø radar gathers data that is important for the American missile shield, but which is not dependent on being sent in "real-time". This is information about Russian tests of intercontinental missiles, which are of decisive significance in regard to whether or not the American missile defense system would be able to function in a genuine situation.

In the genuine situation the following would happen: The intercontinental Russian missile would, after it has attained its planned position, launch the nuclear weapon, which is surrounded by a number of objects to sew doubt with the USA as to which is

---

246
http://www.regjeringen.no/nb/dep/smk/dok/rapporter_planer/rapporter/2005/sori a-moria-erklaringen.html?id=438515
[247] Interview with Espen Barth Eide winter, 2006. Telephone conversation with Kjetil Skogrand, winter 2011.

the right target to react against. This takes place in gravity-free space, which means the decoy weapon could for instance be your common birthday balloons that have the same speed as the nuclear weapon. To be able to differentiate between the real weapon and perhaps 50 decoys, is regarded as one of the biggest challenges to get an intercontinental nuclear missile defense to work. The Vardø radar gathers this type of data from Russian missile tests.

The USA does not like this recently expressed Norwegian skepticism to the missile shield. In 2007 the U.S. Embassy in Oslo applies heavy pressure on leading governmental and parliamentary politicians, research environments and journalists to prevent dissension in NATO on the plans for a European missile shield. Documents from the U.S. Embassy released by WikiLeaks reveal that the embassy has among other things meetings about the matter with the chairman of the Defense Committee, Jan Petersen (H), and the cabinet secretary in the Ministry for Defense, Espen Barth Eide (AP).[248] During a lunch meeting between the U.S. Ambassador Benson K. Whitney and the Minister of Foreign Affairs, Jonas Gahr Støre rejects that the formulation in Soria Moria is a genuine problem for building a European NATO missile shield, according to the report.[249]

Outwardly the Ministry of Defense maintains the critical line. During a meeting of NATO defense ministers in Vilnius on 7th February 2008 the Minister of Defense Anne-Grete Strøm-Erichsen (AP) tells the media that she doubts there is a need for a missile defense system, and that a missile defense system could increase the danger of an arms race.[250] Meanwhile SV's leader, Kristin Halvorsen, says the government's stance remains firm, whether the missile defense system is built under the regime of NATO or the United States. SV says Norway must give thorough consideration to laying down a veto if this should prove necessary.

---

[248] http://www.aftenposten.no/spesial/wikileaksdokumenter/article3972767.ece

[249] http://www.aftenposten.no/spesial/wikileaksdokumenter/article3972763.ece

[250] http://www.dagsavisen.no/innenriks/article334134.ece

The Senterpartiet's spokesman on defense policy, Alf Ivar Samuelsen, is also still saying no to a missile shield.[251]

This takes place while the United States is negotiating an agreement with Poland on placement of ten U.S. missiles on Polish soil that would be able to counterattack intercontinental nuclear missiles attacking the USA and Europe. The United States is also engaged in talks with the Czech authorities about transfer of a radar installation at Kwajalein in the Pacific Ocean to the Czech Republic. This would enable the United States to have its own European missile defense. Russia's president Vladimir Putin is furious, threatening to aim Russian arms at Europe, and announces that this means the world is once again back in the Cold War.[252]

On the other side of the Atlantic Cornell University and Massachusetts Institute of Technology has a research programme investigating how the new American missile defense system in Europe would work in practice. Professor Theodore Postol presents the results in Berlin 29th February 2008 in a lecture at Deutsche Physikalische Gesellschaft, which today has nine Nobel Prize winners amongst its members.[253]

One of two principal finds in the American research is that the only European radar that would be capable of identifying the genuine weapon, and which are decoy weapons in a missile attack from Iran over Greenland toward the west coast of the USA, is the Vardø radar. The planned Czech radar will not have technical capacity for that. Postol says it appears as though the Norwegian authorities still haven't informed the Norwegian population about this crucial role for the Vardø radar.

---

[251] http://www.dagsavisen.no/innenriks/article331618.ece

[252] http://www.foxnews.com/story/0,2933,277492,00.html

[253]
http://russianforces.org/files/BriefOnEastEuropeMissileDefenseProposal_August24,2007_FinalReduced.pdf

Postol and the Assistant Director for the Peace Studies Program at Cornell University, George N. Lewis, repeat these serious allegations in a scientific article published in the renowned American scientific journal Bulletin of the Atomic Scientists[254]. In a press briefing uploaded to the Internet, Postol says that Russian military are without doubt fully aware of the Vardø radar's new significance, and it wouldn't come as any surprise if Norwegian military and politicians also know about the connection.[255]

I find everything on the Internet in the spring and summer of 2008, but not a word about the matter is reported in Norwegian media; it's as silent as the grave. January 2011; I'm on my way from Finnmark to California to meet Postol. I'm eager for him to define the connection between the United States' European missile shield, which in the meantime has also become NATO's missile shield in Europe.

The contrast from the polar night in Finnmark is considerable as I sit on the train to the little town of Palo Alto, a half-hour's journey south of San Francisco. Cactuses tall and green line the railway track and temperatures are the same as a pleasant Norwegian summer. Half the year Postol is attached to Stanford University, which is located just by Palo Alto.

Postol is a highly esteemed researcher. Time after time he has proven he was right in often unpopular standpoints. For instance he whipped up a storm when he revealed how remarkably inaccurate the U.S. Patriot missiles were against the Iraqi Scud missiles during the invasion of Kuwait in 1991. The Pentagon claimed 80 percent of the Scud missiles were hit, while Postol during a hearing in Congress documented that the hit percentage was less than 10. Congress concluded that only a handful of the

---

[254] http://www.thebulletin.org/files/064002009.pdf

[255] http://www.thebulletin.org/content/media-center/announcements/2008/04/30/press-briefing-missile-defense-follow (turn on sound to hear recording of the briefing)

Patriot missiles had hit, and there was little actual evidence to prove any had hit at all.[256]

He meets me at the train station. We proceed to his office, and I switch on my audio recorder. The 64 year old professor still maintains the Vardø radar is totally essential for the U.S. missile defense to function in Europe: "It's very difficult to understand why the Vardø radar would not be employed as a part of the American missile defense system. The reason being that it is the only radar that has any possibility whatsoever of identifying a warhead from a decoy. It is the only radar with a resolution and range that can provide information on what is a warhead and what is a decoy weapon in an attempt to track an intercontinental nuclear missile from Iran to mid-states or the east coast of the USA".

Postol is of the opinion it must be obvious to the Norwegian authorities that the radar has this role, and that the Norwegian population should be informed of this. He also thinks the method of use must be agreed upon between the Norwegian and American authorities. "I have difficulty imagining anything else," he says.

Obama is keen to position land-based SM-3 missiles in Poland and Romania in the period 2015–2020. In May 2011 the United States and Romania enter into an agreement on placement of missiles in Romania. Postol has great sympathy for Russian fears that the new missile defense will be used against Russia – arms that could one day point towards Moscow, not Teheran. Russia's Ambassador Dmitry Rogozin had this to say about a possible cooperation between NATO and Russia after a meeting with NATO on a joint missile shield in Brussels in January 2011: "It cannot be called a cooperation. It isn't even a marriage of convenience. It's like living in different rooms in different apartments, with different entrances and addresses."[257]

---

[256] http://www.dagsavisen.no/utenriks/article486741.ece

[257] http://www.foreignpolicyjournal.com/2011/02/10/the-prospects-for-missile-

Some months later Russia's President Dmitry Medvedev doesn't pull any punches during his first regular press conference in Moscow. He says straight out that the American decision to build the missile shield in the former Eastern Europe despite Russian warnings, will force Moscow to "to take countermeasures – which we would rather not do. We must then look at developing the offensive potential of our nuclear arsenal." The Russian president threatened to pull Russia out of the newly signed START agreement, which would reduce the countries' nuclear arsenal by one-third – a situation with serious consequences:

"This will be an extremely unfortunate scenario. It will be a situation that puts us back on a cold war footing" was Medvedev's comment.[258]

Postol is convinced that Russia knows that only the Vardø radar of all radar installations in Europe has the technical capacity that can be utilized by the Americans to track missiles. The irritation of the Vardø radar is not going to go away for the Russians. Vardø is an obvious potential target for the Russians.

---

defense-cooperation-between-nato-and-russia/

[258]

http://www.nypost.com/p/news/international/russian_president_threatens_return_eA6De6Py9SS6xvq9tTrXUN

Chapter 14
Radar a vital aid in launching space attacks

In my research in connection with the Vardø radar I've understood the Norwegian intelligence service is correct in its remark: The radar does have several tasks. However the intelligence service has not informed fully about what the different tasks are, and what the different data is to be used for. In addition to contributing toward the American missile defense system, the Vardø radar is also important to the United States ability to attack hostile satellites in space.

The company that produced the radar and was in charge of its transfer from the United States to Norway, Raytheon, claims the most important task for the radar after its removal to Norway, is to gather data on "deep-space satellites" – satellites that orbit furthest away from the earth.

This involves gathering data on the around 400 geo-stationary earth observation and communications satellites in an orbit following the earth's rotation, 36 000 kilometers above the equator. Due to the satellites following the earth's rotation, when seen from the earth they will appear at any given time at a fixed point.

Information from Raytheon is in agreement with e-mail contact I have had with the head of the media section at Air Force Space Command headquarters, Angie I. Blair. She writes that the radar was moved from the USA to Norway primarily to monitor satellites in the outer orbits in an area other American radars cannot see.

This area is from 0-meridian to 90 degrees east, which is the longitude from England in the west to Pakistan in the east. As the satellites very high above the earth's surface, the Vardø radar can see the satellite belt above the equator for about one-third of the circumference of the planet.

The area covered by the Vardø radar is confirmed in writing by sources at Hanscom Air Force Base, who were responsible for following up the supplier Raytheon, and also the U.S. Air Force Command and the Armed Forces' research institute.[259] Globus II provided coverage of a crucial strategic area that previously was without coverage.[260]

So why monitor this area? The short answer is that it is a part of the USA's preparations to make space into the new arena for war.

If we delve a little deeper it is perhaps worth reminding the reader about the long-term plan for American military activities in space from 1997, "United States Space Command Vision 2020", which is mentioned in chapter 12. The ambition is quite clearly to make space an integral part of the entire American war machinery:

> U.S. Space Command – military superiority in space in its support of operations that will protect American interests and investments. Building military strength in space into an integral part of the total war effort in all types of conflicts.

Given the increasing economic significance of space, it can only be expected that space – during the course of the first decades after the new millennium becomes a military arena on a par with land, sea and air, according to the plan. Anticipated increased tension between the rich and poor regions of the world necessitates preparations for war in and from space, is the message.

---

[259] http://www.cdi.org/pdfs/Korsbakken.pdf

[260] http://www.fas.org/spp/military/program/track/globusII.pdf, page 7

198

The long-term plan is followed up by a complete, concrete plan of operation two years later, "The U.S. Air Force Command's Strategic Master Plan for FY02 and Beyond". Seen with Norwegian eyes chapter six', "Integrated Phased Plan", is interesting. Particularly the paragraph "Evolve Space Superiority" – on developing dominion of space.

> Gaining space superiority will become as important tomorrow as gaining air superiority is today. In the near-term, we will lay the foundation to gain full space superiority. The primary near-term focus is to improve our space surveillance capabilities. To do so, we will upgrade some of our existing ground-based space surveillance systems such as the Eglin radar and the GEODSS network, add capabilities with the completed relocation and upgrade of GLOBUS II.[261]

It might be interesting to know what the USA means by having dominion over space, and what means would be employed to achieve this dominion.

Two years after this plan of action is presented, in 2004, the U.S. Air Force announces for the first time the guidelines for American warfare in space, "Counterspace Operations, Air Force Doctrine Documents 2-2.1". There it states the USA intends to have dominion or full military control of space, so-called "Space Superiority", which is defined as follows:

> The degree of dominance in space of one force over another that permits the conduct of operations by the former and its related land, sea, air, space, and special operations forces at a given time and place without prohibitive interference by the opposing force.[262]

261

http://www.wslfweb.org/docs/afspaceplan02/CHAPTER%206%20INTEGRAT
ED%20PHASED%20IMPLEMENTATION%20PLAN.htm
[262] http://www.dtic.mil/doctrine/jel/service_pubs/afdd2_2_1.pdf

The same document states that the means to achieve dominion in space is military systems to defend own satellites and to attack hostile satellites. The doctrine states that the USA can also be the first to attack. This would occur in the event of preventing an enemy from 'exploiting space to its advantage' as the phrase goes. In the foreword General John Jumper, Commander-in-Chief of the U.S. Air Force writes:

> Counterspace operations are critical to success in modern warfare. .. The development of offensive counterspace capabilities provides combatant commanders with new tools for counterspace operations. .. These operations may be utilized throughout the spectrum of conflict and may achieve a variety of effects from temporary denial to complete destruction of the adversary's space capability.

The same official document lists a long list of actual offensive military instruments. The Americans are prepared to go to attack on satellites with everything they have from using aircraft with laser weapons and ground-based weapons, to use of own attack satellites. In addition the Americans can launch attacks against an enemy's satellite communications links with the ground, ground stations, and transmission lines to command centers or against launch installations.

Another way to illustrate the Vardø radar's connection to the new American strategy is to look at use of the American military term, Space Situational Awareness, SSA. SSA is defined as all knowledge about all types of objects in space and about weather and other environmental data in space. The U.S. Air Force has a separate item in the budget for 2011 that involves an upgrade of a number of sensors for SSA, including Globus II. It emerges here that as a part of SSA, this includes intelligence about hostile activities in space. The upgrade will among other things provide improved early warning of satellites located above U.S. forces and improved early warning of satellite attacks.[263]

---

263 http://www.dtic.mil/descriptivesum/Y2011/AirForce/0305940F_PB_2011.pdf

200

Winter 2005, and Major Tommy A. Roberts at U.S. Air Force headquarters writes in the in-house magazine for U.S. Air Force Space Command High Frontier that focus is heightened on warfare in space and therefore also on SSA, which is a natural assumption:

While the concept of SSA is certainly not new, the increasing focus on Offensive and Defensive Counterspace (OCS/DCS) has brought an accompanying focus on SSA, since situational awareness is the foundation for any OCS or DCS operation. In simple terms, it is hard to target (OCS) or defend (DCS) assets that you cannot find so the US makes an effort to "find" as much as it can. [264]

Space Situational Awareness also means being in possession of knowledge about what is known as space weather and other types of environmental data. Energy from the sun changes and can disrupt satellite communications, data equipment in GPS satellites and radar signals and make it more difficult to differentiate between a natural phenomenon and a hostile attack. Environmental data can be knowledge concerning the volume of the different types of beams and particles following a nuclear attack in space. [265]

The United States' only space-based military weather forecast system, DMSP, where a number of satellites download data on Svalbard, provides this kind of information. Two new launches are planned for DMSP satellites.

Meanwhile the USA has planned a whole new generation of satellites for military and civilian weather and environmental data, The National Polar-orbiting Operational Environmental Satellite System, NPOESS. In this instance Svalbard was to have been the principal point for downloading of data. This programme was stopped by the Obama administration due to disagreements

---

[264] http://www.afspc.af.mil/shared/media/document/AFD-070622-057.pdf
[265] http://www.afspc.af.mil/shared/media/document/AFD-060524-005.pdf

between military and civilian parties and excessive costs, and is now split into separate civilian and military sections. It is unclear what role Svalsat has now.

A pilot project, NPOESS Preparatory Project, NPP, is proceeding as planned. In January 2011, representatives from NASA Goddard Space Flight and NASA headquarters in Washington give assurance that everything is on schedule for launching of the NPP satellite in autumn of the same year.[266] NPP is a civilian-military satellite that will transfer data about weather and environmental conditions on earth – and in space – via fiber cable from Svalsat to the United States.[267] The military has the ambition to provide ten times more detail in downloads of weather and environmental data and speeding up downloads of the same by up to five times more than is currently the case.

This type of knowledge is also important for reliable information from radar systems such as the Vardø radar. Good weather and environmental data simplify the job for the Vardø radar in tracking a hostile satellite, and to detect whether the signals will be disrupted by a change in the amount of electrically charged particles between the radar and the satellite.[268] Installations that are utilized to ensure the United States dominion over space complement each other, whether they are in Finnmark, Svalbard, Antarctica or other places.

I travel to Montreal to meet Brian Weeden, who until 2007 was an air force captain stationed in the U.S. Space Command, 1st Space Control Squadron, deep in the bedrock in Colorado. His job consisted of analyzing data from Globus II and other American sensors across the globe. Brian Weeden also built up and headed the training of all employees in the unit designated for space analysis. The former officer was previously in charge of the

---

[266] http://www.prnewswire.com/news-releases/nasas-npp-satellite-undergoing-flight-environmental-testing-115969109.html
[267] http://www.ipo.noaa.gov/instruments/C3_Segment.pdf

[268] See note 265

launching of intercontinental nuclear missiles from underground bunkers at Malmstrom AFB Base in Montana.

He now lives in Montreal and works as a researcher for Secure World Foundation, which is one of the cutting-edge American independent expertise centers for space security policy. Working within the Colorado underground base were also Canadians, as part of the Canadian-American collaboration on North American defense. There Brian met Canadian Charity, and it was love and a new baby that led Brian to leave the U.S. Armed Forces to start a career in research in Canada.

This morning I'm standing freezing on a sidewalk outside my hotel in a busy city street in Montreal waiting for Brian. I'm used to the cold in Finnmark, but not the Canadian cold. It's only minus 15 Celsius, but evaporation from lakes and rivers create extreme humidity and frost penetrates marrow and bone alike, even though I am wearing thick winter clothing from home in Norway.

To make things worse, Brian Weeden has not turned up at the agreed time. Have I travelled here to no avail? I shuffle back and forth on the sidewalk in an effort to keep warm.

The flight from California to Montreal took ten hours. It would appear a somewhat expensive waste of time. I try to be patient, and finally he shows up, as jovial and round as I have seen in photos. He fishes out an iPhone and finds a lunch bar close by where we can eat and talk. Naturally he has his young son as the screen image on his mobile.

Food is not foremost in my mind. I take out various documents I've found on the Internet I want to show him, switch on an audio recorder and make sure it is working. I'm aware I'm in a 'geared' state and perhaps rather stressed out by the fact I'm sitting at a table with a former U.S. Air Force captain, whose daily activity until recently consisted of working with the Vardø radar. He is very candid about the Vardø radar's tasks:

In order to monitor satellites high above the equator there are three radar systems. These are the Vardø radar together with the Millstone installations near Boston in Massachusetts and the Reagan experimental station on the Kwajalein Islands in the Pacific Ocean that have the Altair radar, Alcor and Tradex. These three systems cover the belt of satellites above the equator around the entire planet. The radar systems track the satellites as well as space debris in this area.

From the top of Vårberget in Vardø the radar transmits its signals southwards over the Varangerfjord, across northern Russia, Sweden and Finland, upwards into the heavens. With the aid of positions that the Norwegian intelligence people in Vardø have received from their colleagues in California, the signals are transmitted to satellites orbiting high above Africa and Asia before they return to Finnmark in cryptic form. On the other side table from me sits a man who until recently worked with the radar system on a daily basis.

"The Joint Space Operations Center is the name of the American military organization that is responsible for monitoring everything in space. This organization produces a daily list for all sensors, whether it be Vardø, Haystack or others. Then it's up to the sensors to find solutions to their tasks. Observations over the equator can be made anywhere; observations in space above the station must be made when the objects pass above. There can also be supplementary tasks. For instance, a radar might detect the launch of a satellite, and we attempt to track it," says Weeden.

In Norway and abroad the discussion on the Vardø radar has been connected to missile defense system. Weeden is of the opinion that the Vardø radar plays a major role in America's space defense efforts.

"I don't know whether that was the most important reason it was moved to Norway. I wasn't involved in making that decision. But in my experience having the Vardø radar in that part of the world and being able to cover sections of Europe and Asia is

204

very, very important for space surveillance and space defense", he says.

He goes on to say that the United States has satellites above the equator, spread across the globe, which monitor missile launches, both those that are potentially capable of reaching the USA, and short-range missiles that are employed in regional conflicts. It is especially important to keep a close eye on satellites that hang over the regions that encompass the conflicts in the Middle East and Afghanistan. "If you are to defend these satellites, you must have a sensor such as Globus that can track satellites in the vicinity, see whether other satellites are closing in, whether it is space debris in the area or an attack on the satellite."

It's an almost obvious conclusion to draw that it's first and foremost the combination of the location of Vardø's easterly location and capability to monitor areas of unrest in Asia and Europe, together with the capability of tracking test launches and firings of Russian intercontinental rockets and nuclear missiles from Plesetsk and the Barents Sea at close proximity that is the main reason why the Pentagon plumped for Vardø. Weeden thinks the Vardø radar would provide vital information in an outbreak of hostilities in space.

"Much of the same type of information from the Vardø radar that is important for defense of our satellites is also crucial for engaging in an attacking war. In both instances the foremost priority is to have information about positions of objects, their orbits and velocity. The position can be used for both defense and attack," says Weeden.

He believes it is highly likely that in the next major conflict the USA has with another state, at least one of the parties will try to strike the counterpart's satellites. Weeden thinks such a situation could easily lead to a war on the ground escalating to a full-on war in space. In his opinion the world is in a dangerous stage of development.

"Just recently India has been talking about having its own missile defense system and assault weapons against satellites. The reason that the country has said this publicly is because they want to scare off other nations from attacking Indian satellites. We are seeing a spreading of this hit-to-kill-technology used to attack satellites and for missile defense systems that has been dispersed from the USA and Russia to countries such as China, India and potentially to other countries. There are no agreements that prohibit or prevent such testing or development. And countries like the United States don't want such agreements."

So says Brian Weeden. A few days later I'm sitting on a plane from the USA flying over Greenland, en route on my last trip. In the half-light of dusk I gaze down at the clouds. The aircraft is cruising at an altitude of 10 000 meters. It's five times this distance up to the satellites that are closest to the earth. As I view the cloud 'landscape' below me, I am reminded of Man's conquest of the skies that commenced around one hundred years ago, and the conquest of space that all started 50 years ago with the launch of the Russian satellite Sputnik.

Sitting beside me is an 18–19 year old German who has just spent a long weekend in San Francisco visiting his girlfriend. A computer expert, originally from South Korea and formerly resident in Helsinki, is on his way to London to hold a course. Aviation has become a natural part of the modern, global community, both civilian and military. But how often does conversation turn to how satellite and space technology are now revolutionizing the entire world community?

The global economy can survive air traffic coming to a complete standstill for a few days; not so with an equally long halt for satellite activity, due to the satellites' importance for money transfers and communications. So said John Kristian Skogan, researcher at the Norwegian Institute of International Affairs (NUPI) and former cabinet secretary in the Ministry of Defense, to me a couple of years ago. Perhaps it is true to say that aviation spent the first 50 years of the last century to make itself indispensable to the global community, while at least equally

206

important has been the development of satellite activities and other space activities the last 50 years? At least as far as the civilian community is concerned.

Ronald Reagan scared a whole world in the eighties with his visions of Star Wars. But now it emerges this work never ceased. The Americans spend more money on their missile shield than any other arms system in any country ever. As a part of this the American radar in Vardø plays a vital role, despite the Norwegian government's assurances that this is not the case. The Americans will also utilize the Vardø radar in regular aggressive warfare in space. I have just learned other countries are responding and consolidating their armed defenses.

Last century we were used to distinguishing between war fought in the air and on the ground. With this century, will we distinguish between battles fought in the air, on the ground AND in space? Is it an absolute must for Norway to be a crucial contributor?

The Norwegian government is the initiative-taker to the Nansen–Amundsen Year 2011, which is a national marking of the 150 years since Fridtjof Nansen was born and 100 years since the Norwegian expedition headed by Roald Amundsen was the first to reach the South Pole. It might seem strange to combine two such different jubilees, but the common denominator is proud Norwegian polar traditions. How do we manage this inheritance? Would Fridtjof Nansen, Nobel Peace Prize winner for his efforts to combat and halt widespread death amongst the population from starvation in Siberia and other places, have been in favor of Norway allowing use of Svalbard for warfare, which is directly in conflict with a binding international agreement?

One of the very few statues in Vardø is of Fridtjof Nansen, erected after he sailed from Vardø in 1893 with the expedition vessel "Fram" in the direction of the North Pole. Would Nansen, a stalwart champion of Norwegian independence, have appreciated that Vardø – one hundred years later – is being used as the spearhead for American militarization of space, even though Norway – at least officially – is against such a turn of events?

It's 14th December 2011. The Norwegian flag flutters in the wind at the South Pole – 100 years to the day after Roald Amundsen's expedition – as the first ever – reached the South Pole. According to plan, Prime Minister Jens Stoltenberg attends and underlines the national significance of the jubilee. Should we be equally proud that we operate a satellite station on the 'peaceful continent' that in an ever-increasing role serves areas of conflict all over the world? How are we to manage our polar inheritance? Is this the kind of progress we want? Does anybody in Parliament really care anyway?

Notes

The websites in the notes were visited in June 2011.

E-mail author: baaworm@online.no webpage book:
www.facebook.com/satellittkrigen
Coverphoto: Canada Space Agency

Made in United States
Cleveland, OH
28 June 2025

18089121R00118